D0056388

EVE

EVE

AND THE

MORTAL
JOURNEY

Finding Wholeness,
Happiness, and Strength

BEVERLY CAMPBELL

**DESERET
BOOK**
SALT LAKE CITY, UTAH

Visit us at deseretbook.com

Library of Congress Cataloging-in-Publication Data

   Campbell, Beverly (Beverly Brough)
   Eve and the mortal journey : finding wholeness, happiness, and strength / Beverly Campbell.
       p. cm.
   Includes bibliographical references and index.
   ISBN 1-59038-397-4 (alk. paper) 3296 6581 4/06
   1. Eve (Biblical figure)   2. Church of Jesus Christ of Latter-day Saints—Doctrines.   3. Mormon Church—Doctrines.   4. Christian life—Mormon authors.   I. Title.
   BX8643.E92C37 2005
   248.4'89332—dc22
                                                                           2004026432

Printed in the United States of America   18961
R. R. Donnelley and Sons, Crawfordsville, IN

10   9   8   7   6   5   4   3   2

To Lenore, Dessa, Cloe, Arlene, Ursel,
Betty, Marilyn, Virginia, Vilma,
Jessie, Ann, Fay, Linda, and Ariel
sisters, sisters-in-law, and more than sisters
who have shared and enriched my life

To my myriad of nieces and grandnieces
who live with such promise

To the Janies, Alycias, Cyndis, Shauris, and Heathers
who dedicate their lives and talents
to those things of import in the kingdom

We have not been sent
to endlessly investigate the darkness
but rather to seek divine light
and to walk in that resplendent light

CONTENTS

PREFACE

As work on my earlier book, *Eve and the Choice Made in Eden,* was coming to a close, I came to realize that the lessons of Eden provide a reality-based life text for each of us. The principles revealed in the Garden story provide syllabus, model, and map for our journey through mortality. What happened in Eden not only illuminates but also informs the daily business of living richly woven, joy-filled, purposeful lives—challenging and sorrow-etched though they may be at times. And then I realized: "Of course, that is what God intended that example to be."

In the premortal councils, you and I and everyone who has lived, now lives, or will yet live on earth were taught and accepted that plan that is called the Great Plan of Happiness. Surely, with the clear vision that existed in that sphere, we must have recognized the challenges that would confront us in mortality. But the opportunity to claim a mortal body and the hope of at last obtaining eternal life made it all worthwhile.

Some, because of circumstances or lack of light, feel that they have been thrust into a lonely, dark world without rudder or compass. Yet the first recorded question God asks Adam and Eve after they have partaken of the fruit of mortality is, "Where goest thou?" (Moses 4:15). Quo vadis? What path take you? The Lord seems to be asking, "Have you got your bearings—do you know where you need to go, and do you know what you need to do when you get there?"

Then He set this dear, tender young couple, the first of His mortal children, on a path *eastward*.

Biblical scholars tell us that such an *eastward* movement "ensures that the student of scripture will perceive the Fall as the positive and divinely foreordained event that it was."[1] As the door closes on Eden, Adam and Eve are directed in their footsteps by a loving God "along the only path that would prepare them for eternal glory,"[2] for symbolically, when one moves *eastward* one is moving toward the face of God.

Upon our entry into mortality, the internal compass in each of us is set in that same direction, *east,* toward the face of God. Along with that compass setting comes an absolute and glorious promise from the Lord himself:

"I will go before your face.

"I will be on your right hand and on your left,

"And my spirit shall be in your hearts,

"And mine angels round about you, to bear you up." (D&C 84:88)

EASTWARD ORIENTATION

Let us talk a little about the rich and instructive theological significance of that eastward path on which we are set as we enter mortality. A Hebrew word commonly used for *east* literally means the place of sunrise.[3] In the biblical Greek, east and sunrise mean the same thing, thus the words used evoke images of a new dawn, of hope, of beginnings. The New Testament speaks of the sending forth of God's glory like the dawn that breaks forth from the east, or as the sun that sheds light on all the inhabitants of the earth.

The scriptures are replete with these themes of resplendent light, eternal and absolute love, and assured orientation.[4] The Savior declares himself to be "the light of the world" (D&C 11:28) and says that His return shall be "out of the east" (Matthew 24:27). We see God's word as light, God's thoughts as enlightenment.[5]

THERE IS A PLAN FOR YOUR LIFE

It is my belief that there is not only purpose to every life but a plan for every life. Each plan is individual and encompasses the challenges, trials, and opportunities that will provide wholeness and happiness for that individual. I also believe that sufficient light and strength is provided for the journey one might embrace and for the completion of those missions agreed to in heavenly councils.

Interestingly, in those councils where we embraced all of this, we also accepted that as we entered mortality, a veil would be drawn over our eyes providing little recall of those earlier scenes, so that we might be tested while living by faith. That veil makes it difficult in the process of day-to-day living to see the purpose or the shape of one's whole life. Sometimes, however, after a long season has passed, we can look back and see a pattern. We recognize a series of directions taken, opportunities seized, and challenges embraced, and we understand that what we have been about is not really entirely of our making. Out of the mist emerges evidence of a divine and loving hand, which has generously prepared, carefully nurtured, and truly guided us along paths we would never have chosen and tutored us in ways that have required us to move beyond our perceived capacities.

In the following chapters there are examples of such occurrences in the lives of others; however, a request came to me after all was written that I describe also some of the ways my life has been so directed and used. While I find it hard to talk about myself in such personal ways, I would be remiss if I did not acknowledge the incredible gifts God has given me and the tutorials he prepared that I might fulfill that which I was called to do.

From the vantage point of time, I can see that my entire life encompasses a series of events that have required me to stretch in ways I might not have chosen and to develop talents and capabilities I would not have claimed, all directed by a generous and loving God who has used me in ways I would never have imagined.

To begin, I had never intended to have a career beyond

the hope of being a loving partner, an excellent wife, a good mother, an imaginative homemaker, and a sure and steady daughter of God. But events pushed me out into the world in ways I hadn't anticipated, raising challenges that were at times excruciating and propelling me into positions I could not have foreseen. In the early years, my work outside the home was done out of necessity, and in the later years out of desire and dedication.

Let us fast-forward to 1979. There was a national debate raging over a proposed amendment to the Constitution of the United States. The so-called Equal Rights Amendment had stirred up great feelings pro and con, and debates on television and radio and in the newspapers were intense and divisive. On the face of it, it sounded reasonable and desirable—to secure equal rights under the law for both men and women. But as I studied the amendment, I came to feel that it would codify a doctrine of *sameness* rather than *equality* between men and women, and I determined I could not support it.

We were living in Washington, D.C., at that time, and I was approached by several groups who favored the amendment, asking me to join with them. I responded that I would be unable to do so; however, I remember saying to a friend, "I hope I am never asked to articulate why I am against such an amendment because it would be very hard to make it clear."

As the debate intensified, I saw the need to be actively engaged in advancing legitimate concerns, lest the amendment be passed. The Church of Jesus Christ of Latter-day

Saints, along with other entities, had expressed its opposition to the amendment. With a group of other like-minded friends, some LDS, some not, we began to do what we could to communicate our concerns to our representatives in the Virginia State Legislature, who had the bill before them. We hoped any inequalities between men and women might be handled in ways other than a constitutional amendment.

One afternoon, as my husband, Pierce, and I were packing to move into a new home, I received a call from Church headquarters, asking if I would take a plane that night to Chicago to appear on the *Phil Donahue Show* the next day with a well-known proponent of the ERA cause. (This show was the *Oprah* of that day, and the host was vocally pro ERA.) If there was anything in my life I did not want to do, nor felt prepared to do, it was that. However, I had made covenants with the Lord that I would help at anytime and anywhere I was needed in the kingdom, and so with great trepidation, I said yes.

As a result of that experience, I was asked thereafter to become a spokesperson for the Church on this and other women's issues, and for the next two years, I traveled extensively in this assignment, doing hundreds of radio and print interviews and appearing on television in many states. (History shows that the amendment was ultimately defeated and that the laws that were needed to ensure equality between men and women were passed without amending the Constitution.)

Was this what I wanted to do? No. Did I feel prepared?

No. Did I feel the presence of the adversary at every turn? Yes. Did I know of God's hand in it? Absolutely. Could I have done it had I not earlier been pushed out into very visible positions, which had given me confidence and authority? Probably not. Was there a cost? Certainly. Many of my former associates, friends, and business interests in Washington, D.C. withdrew from me. Was there a reward? Without question! Those experiences taught me to trust in the Lord, and they gave me a sure testimony of the doctrine of divine guidance and of the wisdom granted to those called by God to positions of responsibility.

Out of these experiences came relationships that were preparatory to my next mission. As I accepted other assignments, fulfilled other duties, worked with priesthood leaders throughout the Eastern seaboard and at Church headquarters, I grew exponentially. My media contacts were put to good use, my speaking directed to other issues, concerns, and causes. My interest in international affairs and love of international travel were exercised to the fullest.

Then, as if to prove there is never advancement without a time of terrible testing, our daughter's life was taken in a senseless accident during a time when my husband and I were traveling abroad.

Amid this blackness and mourning came another telephone call, asking if I would take an assignment to establish an office that could help advance the purposes of the Church on an international level. Specific instruction was not provided, but I was given an opportunity to shape and refine ways to open the doors to nations where the Church was not recognized or where we had not previously been admitted. For the work to go forward in these countries, the Church would need official recognition, permission for members to gather, and freedom for our missionaries to enter or remain in those nations. Because anything is possible with the Lord, I was confident we could succeed, with the support of wonderful priesthood leaders who were also CEOs of major corporations, members of Congress, and men of authority and influence.

Thus began the privilege of working with members of the Quorum of the Twelve Apostles, who have responsibility for the international Church. Our home in Washington, D.C., became an "embassy" for the Church, where dinners and meetings were frequently held with all the key players. Ambassadors came to call me friend and address me as "Mrs. Ambassador."

Many miracles occurred as we worked behind the Iron Curtain, in the African nations, and with our friends in the Orient. The relationships, and indeed friendships, which were developed over time now range throughout the world and have enriched and enlivened our lives in all ways. My husband, Pierce, was at my side in full support at every step. After twelve plus years in this work, during which I served as Director of International Affairs for the Church, I completed my fourth unintended career.

As I look back, a clear pattern emerges. I realize that every experience I've had throughout my life—every trial, challenge, and career opportunity, and the capabilities and drive I developed, which allowed me to move forward, were the result of pretraining I had received, not in this sphere, but before ever coming here. These traits were given life by my willingness to accept the challenges, do the hard work and preparatory study, try that which was untried, go the extra mile, and above all to believe in and accept that all things are possible when one is walking with the matchless love, support, and comfort of her own beloved Savior and those called to guide His church here on earth.

And now I have the privilege of taking the experiences and the wisdom thus gleaned and putting them on paper. My hope is that what I have learned will benefit you in your own journey *eastward* and encourage you to lay claim to your own blessings as you pursue your earthly missions.[6]

1

Longings of the Soul, Desires of the Heart

I long to know God's thoughts—for there is light.
I long to feel God's love—for there is peace.
I long to hear God's voice—for there is home.
I long to move ever Eastward.

Have you ever been utterly homesick for the Spirit, not fully aware of what it is you are seeking or missing, yet feeling desolate and alone? Such must have been the emotions of our first parents, Adam and Eve, upon finding themselves in mortality. They had walked and talked with God amid all that was beautiful, peaceful, and holy. In this new sphere, they were disoriented. They found themselves subject to new emotions. They felt loss, loneliness, confusion. They were homesick for His light, for His Spirit. So many in this world are similarly affected, yet cannot identify the source of the longing, so know not where to go for redress.

My first real bout with such spiritual homesickness occurred in my eighteenth year. My friend Emily and I had embarked on a journey, quite extraordinary for two young women at that period of history. Determined to see a bit of the world, we found a couple who needed their new Oldsmobile convertible driven to their new assignment in Washington, D.C. Since this was to be our first real adventure, we wanted to sample as many of those places we had read about as time and itinerary would allow.

The first leg of our journey took us through the heartland of this great country. We thrilled at crossing the Mississippi River. In fact, we turned around, crossed over and back again that we might re-savor the moment. Having been used to the high mountain desert of Utah, we were not prepared for the lush green carpet presented by the burgeoning fields of spring in those vast, flat middle lands. By week's end, however, we were longing for something of home.

We changed our route to be in Nauvoo, Illinois, as soon as possible. Rushing to the temple site, we were surprised to find it empty. Those few people to whom we identified ourselves weren't welcoming. After exploring the historic buildings of that town, so core to our Latter-day Saint history, we returned again to the temple site. As daylight began to fade, we were two lone girls seated on remnants of glory, now reduced to rubble inside the temple's destroyed perimeter walls. Rather than feeling awful, deserted, and disoriented, we were filled with awe and felt secure in our orientation, embraced as we were by the wonder and spirit we felt in that holy place. We spent the hours of sunset into dark retelling the stories of tragedy and sacrifice experienced by our own ancestors and others who had built that magnificent testament to faith and had then had to leave it amid a trail of tears. We wept too. Our tears were tears of thanksgiving, however. All vestiges of homesickness were gone.

We traveled on through Canada, absorbed in the architecture, sounds, and even the signage. After a few days, we were anxious to move on to Palmyra, New York. Our fervent desire was to visit the home believed to be the one in which Joseph Smith received a visit from the angel Moroni, who told him of the Book of Mormon plates, and to see the Sacred Grove where God the Father revealed Himself and His son Jesus the Christ to a praying, trusting, believing Joseph. We were, again, utterly homesick for the Spirit, since we had found no place to attend church on the previous Sunday. The missionary couple attending to the property allowed us to sleep in that room identified as Joseph's. The comfort brought by being in that room and in walking, meditating, and praying in the Sacred Grove had assuaged all new sense of homesickness. We had our orientation back.

Our journey took us on to New York City and a totally unexpected but glorious stay in a suite at the Plaza Hotel, made possible by a kindly hotel clerk who was concerned that two young women on a limited budget, arriving in New York City at nine o'clock on the eve of Easter, would not find another place to stay. We had lingered too long in Palmyra and had lost our assigned reservations.

Other adventures throughout the remainder of our journey were equally amazing, filled with more wonderful "firsts"—visits to the Statue of Liberty, the Empire State Building, Broadway plays, the U.S. Capitol and the White House, the rolling hills of Virginia, the horse country of Kentucky—oh, so much of richness, history, beauty, and just plain fun. However, upon returning home, the things we wished most to share with family were the experiences of temple and grove. The place where I wanted to walk and reflect about the trip was on the grounds of the Salt Lake Temple, which was just one block from my home of that period and which served as a glorious "front yard." From this I learned an important lesson: No matter how grand the adventure or how stunning the diversions, the real, bottom-line longings of the soul, the truest desires of the heart, are to return to those places where we can feel His Spirit. There is home!

> NO MATTER HOW GRAND THE ADVENTURE OR HOW STUNNING THE DIVERSIONS, THE REAL, BOTTOM-LINE LONGINGS OF THE SOUL, THE TRUEST DESIRES OF THE HEART, ARE TO RETURN TO THOSE PLACES WHERE WE CAN FEEL HIS SPIRIT.

A REACHING TOWARD

We should not be surprised that our yearning is toward the divine, that our real orientation is toward things of the Spirit, for we are first and foremost spiritual beings. We are not only away from home, just as were the mortal Adam and Eve, but we are speaking a language that is unfamiliar and that will not assuage the ache in our hearts to hear our mother tongue. The poignant words of our great hymn express it well:

> O my Father, thou that dwellest
> In the high and glorious place,
> When shall I regain thy presence
> And again behold thy face?[1]

More than wishing, more than desiring, more than longing, there is a searching, a searching to find real answers to those greatest of all questions: Who am I, really? Is there some purpose to this life? Where will I go when I leave my mortal body? So many are wandering as though alone in a bleak desert, little understanding that they are hardwired with a compass setting taking them eastward, toward our Heavenly Father, toward home. While it is literally true that we are strangers from a more exalted sphere, God's thoughts, His love, and His voice are ever available to us. He intends that our relationship to Him be a deeply intimate and personal relationship. In His infinite kindness and wisdom as revealed through the restored gospel, He has oriented us perfectly on planet Earth by answering with clarity the three great questions with which most mortals struggle.

Based on restored knowledge, one can say with absolute confidence: I am a child of God. I came from a heavenly home where I was well trained, where I developed strengths and talents that I bring with me here. I am here to gain a mortal body. I am here to claim His promises of happiness and wholeness. I am here to choose, by, of, and for myself, good over evil and thus become as the gods. I am here to make good on those "divine contracts" I entered into in the premortal world. I am here to make sacred, eternally binding covenants, and I have been blessed with the gift of agency, not only to *make* but to choose to *keep* those covenants. Through a Savior and by His atonement, I have every hope of laying claim to eternal life. I will again see His face. I will again hear His voice. *Hallelujah!*

The Language of the Soul

Hallelujah indeed! Declarations of the good news of the gospel seem always to conclude with a chorus of hallelujahs. We understand the joy expressed by the heavenly host that exulted in the birth of Jesus Christ (see Luke 2:13–14). We thrill to the Magnificat of Mary (see Luke 1:46–55) and the expressions of praise found in the book of Psalms. We identify with Eve's (see Moses 5:11) and Elisabeth's (see Luke 1:41–45) paeans of joy heralding the love and mercies of God. We revel in sacred music that brings us nearer to God, whether it is rendered by a magnificent choir, in a soaring aria, by a quiet guitar strumming "I Need Thee Every Hour" in the loneliness and solitude of a starless night, or by a lone voice singing "A Poor Wayfaring Man of Grief" in a melancholy prison cell where a prophet is to be martyred. Our souls resonate to each of these contacts with the Spirit. And oh, how great are the desires of each heart to be clothed again in His glory, to be in tune with the Spirit.

I have always sensed that music is somehow synonymous with the language of heaven. One of my first and most pronounced memories is as a child of three or four when I would hear some distant strain of glorious music. I would run as fast as I could toward that sound. My heart would beat faster and inside was a fear that those beckoning, magnificent tones might end before I got there.

My early years were spent in a small town in Wyoming. In that setting, great musical artists were not available to me, and phonograph players and records were just too expensive. Occasionally, a movie house might have an offering that would feature the music of Chopin or Tchaikovsky or Grieg. I would beg to be taken, not once but as many times as possible. I would watch the film and as one starving would attempt to commit the sounds to memory against some later time of famine. Decades later as I hear a phrase of wonderful music in the distance, I find that same unbidden panic welling inside. Again I fear the strains will stop before I reach them.

A few years ago, my husband and I traveled to Beijing, China. Our business was official. This trip, after months of working with the Chinese ambassador and other key embassy officials in Washington, D.C., and with key "in country" leaders, would culminate in two of our Apostles and other Church dignitaries being received by the vice premier of that great nation. Although all the members of the LDS delegation had been to that country before, this would be the first time leaders of the Church would be received at that level in their official capacity as Apostles of The Church of Jesus Christ of Latter-day Saints. Meetings were also planned with Chinese ministers of education, health, religion, culture, and other departments.

Preparatory work required my husband and me to arrive a few days early. After a long day of meetings, I suggested to our governmental hosts, who we had come to know and love through years of interaction, that there might be some cultural event we could attend. Ever generous and willing to please, a dear young woman was dispatched. She came back with tickets to what was termed an evening of "Western Folk Music." This was not what I had hoped to hear in China, but since all was set in motion, we went.

Ushered into front row center seats, we were the only Westerners I could see. The theater was packed, with even standing room filled. *My*, I thought, *folk music is a real draw here.* Then a full symphony orchestra took the stage, followed by a sixty-voice chorus. The strains of one great aria followed another as the introductions were played. Six of the finest tenors I have heard sang the great musical classics of the Western world. Bravos came unbidden from my throat. Seated on the front row and in such close proximity to the musicians, and so obviously enjoying their offering, I sensed a bond of mutual appreciation being forged between my husband and me and the orchestra and singers. We were not alone in our enjoyment. The audience would not let the performers leave. The tenor who had sung "O Sole Mio," a particular favorite of the audience, had, in my mind, outshone Carreras. We joined in calling for his return. Thinking he had left the theater, the orchestra and chorus began a reprise. Then, from backstage a voice soared over the orchestra long before its owner appeared. Caught in the amid of changing into street clothes, the magnificent singer was still buttoning his shirt as he returned to the stage. More encores were sung, providing a glorious culmination to the concert.

Flushed with pleasure, we joined our hosts for a delightful after-concert dinner, warm with sharing and inclusion. When we returned late to our hotel, we found performing in the open lounge members of the orchestra and a soloist and some of the chorus from the earlier concert. We learned that with the introduction of a market economy in China, each artist was expected to earn "hard dollars" to augment his own salary and that our hotel was the "best gig in town." We sat at a table to listen and quietly feasted again. Some of the musicians recognized us and began to play an aria from *Aida,* which we had so obviously enjoyed earlier. For the remainder of our visit, no matter how filled the day was with meetings or the evening with dinners and events, we rushed back to the hotel at the day's conclusion in hopes of enjoying more of their music. Each night, when they caught sight of us, they would play "our song." It is unlikely that I will forget the historic and awesome events of that trip, which are stories for another day. As well, I will never forget the joy that music brought or the bonds of friendship it engendered.

I have often reflected on this series of events and likened it to how I will likely feel when I hear the welcoming choruses of heaven. Occasionally, I am certain that I hear God's voice from the wings, soaring over the chorus of my life. In my mind's eye, I see Him bursting onto the stage in all His glory. Imagining such, I am awed and humbled, yet an unbidden fear wells in my heart. What if *all* I get to hear is the reprise and then because of something I have done or failed to do, that magnificent voice and munificent presence disappears from my ears, from my sight? What if He is lost to me? What if I am not worthy to be in His presence? Fearing such a possibility, I feel as though my heart will break—absolutely.

DESIRES OF THE HEART

Why do we say in our moments of extreme anguish that we fear our hearts will break? Have you ever noted how often the word *heart* is used in connection with tender emotions and moving events? We speak of having "heavy hearts," coming "heart in hand," enjoying or enduring "affairs of the heart."

Elder Russell M. Nelson, who was a world-renowned heart surgeon before being called to his apostolic office, writes of the wonder that is our heart: "To control the direction of flow of blood within it, there are four important valves, pliable as a parachute and delicate as a dainty silk scarf. They open and close more than one hundred thousand times a day—over thirty-six million times a year. . . . Each day it pumps enough fluid to fill a 2,000 gallon tank."[2] Truly miraculous! Yet, I have always sensed that, impressive as it is, there is something more to the heart than its magnificent life-sustaining function.

We learn from one Bible dictionary that in more than three hundred instances where the word *heart* appears in holy writ, it refers not to the physical organ but to a spiritual condition and to a person's relationship with God. Metaphorically, it is with the heart that one believes, and the heart is that place wherein all that we are is hidden up and can be accessed by God at any time, for though "man looketh on the outward appearance, . . . the Lord looketh on the heart" (1 Samuel 16:7). We are commanded to serve God with all our heart (see Joshua 22:5); we are reminded of the importance of having clean hands and a pure heart (see Psalm 24:4); and we are warned that we will be judged by what is in our heart (see Proverbs 17:3). We read that the Spirit discerned the intents of their heart (see Acts 5:1–10). We also read of hearts filled with pride, with anger, with hatred, about hearts being deluded or deceived, and of hearts of stone and hearts of flesh. We read of a world in the days of Noah where the thoughts of the hearts of almost all inhabiting the earth were continually evil (see Genesis 6:5). Jesus reminded us of the blessedness of the pure in heart (see Matthew 5:8), and most importantly we are assured of the Savior's power and willingness to heal a broken heart: "He healeth the broken in heart, and bindeth up their wounds" (Psalm 147:3).

We know that the heart is that place where we receive sure knowledge. When things are known by the Spirit, it is to the heart that such knowledge comes and thereafter resides. We are commanded to seek God with all our heart.

Our testimonies are manifest by a burning in the bosom (see D&C 9:8). To be truly converted to the gospel, its truths must be written upon our hearts (see Romans 10:9–10), and to have a broken heart and a contrite spirit is the beginning of true repentance (see 3 Nephi 9:20). It appears therefore, that the heart is the seat of spirituality and also the key to our successful earthly relationships, creativity, leadership, happiness, and righteous desires.

WHAT ARE THE DESIRES OF YOUR HEART?

Desire is active, not passive. It has to do with more than wishing; it's about heartfelt longing, and it's about a real craving. Desire by its very nature places priority of one thing over another. We must desire peace above power; we must desire love above lust; we must desire wholeness above gratification. We must desire God's words above man's words. Then we must learn to love those traits that we desire. Unless we work to implement and integrate those holy desires fully into our lives, we cede our power to control them. Desires, like all things in our lives, must be directed, managed, and controlled.

A desire for diversion, undirected, can become a desire for sin. A desire for wealth can become a desire for ill-gotten gain. A desire to win can become a desire to win at any cost. A desire to be held in love can become love held hostage by desire. A desire to be a gourmet can become gluttony. A desire to be totally "laid back" can become a life without purpose. A desire to fit in can become a desire to keep our beliefs and faith undercover. All these desires are imprinted on our heart and not only shape our choices and therefore our lives, but they also become a permanent part of that recording in our heart, which can and will be read by the Lord, just as surely as you are reading the words imprinted on this page.

What is written on your heart? Does it please you? If what is written in your heart at present does not please you, by your desires, choices, and actions, you can overwrite the old and write new messages, which will bring you joy and which are pleasing to the Lord.

Be ever aware that righteous desires need to be relentless, for unrighteous desires will be even more so. As Brigham Young cautions, "The men and women, who desire to obtain seats in the celestial kingdom, will find that they must battle every day."[3] Hence, if one wishes to win the battles of the heart, or of desires, both positive and negative, one must be a full-time warrior.

To be such a warrior will take a lifetime of alert attentiveness to God's words, to His love, and to His voice. It will require that we not only desire to know God but that with that knowledge we desire also to be good and then that we choose to *do* good. We may desire to give love, but we then must choose to extend a divine love, not unconditional but godly and godlike.

Happily, we are assured that even a spark of desire can initiate change. Desire acted upon is choice empowered. It is also encouraging to note that not only our performances but our desires are taken into account by a merciful God. He will factor in the degree of difficulty our varied circumstances impose upon us and not judge us unjustly. "For I, the Lord, will judge all men according to their works, according to the desire of their hearts" (D&C 137:9).

THAT WHICH WE HAVE CHOSEN IS THAT WHICH WE WILL RECEIVE

Alma said: "I know that [God] granteth unto men according to their desire" (Alma 29:4). There is no question that that which we intensely desire over time will be what we eventually will become. We are also assured that that which we have desired with all our hearts here on earth is that which we will receive in the eternities. Elder Neal A. Maxwell teaches us: "In the next world, we will finally receive what we have persistently desired and chosen during mortality. . . . Individually, we will have made so many incontestable, on-the-record choices. The final outcome, therefore, will be perfectly just, and all mortals will so acknowledge. . . . In effect, we will receive the degree of joy we have demonstrably chosen and which we have developed the capacity to receive."[4]

That concept is confirmed in Doctrine & Covenants 88:22–24: "For he who is not able to abide the law of a celestial kingdom cannot abide a celestial glory. And he who cannot abide the law of a terrestrial kingdom cannot abide a terrestrial glory. And he who cannot abide the law of a telestial kingdom cannot abide a telestial glory; therefore he is not meet for a kingdom of glory. Therefore he must abide a kingdom which is not a kingdom of glory."

Thus it would seem that at the resurrection, when our bodies and spirits are again united, never again to be separated, we will receive that body we lived to receive (see 1 Corinthians 15:40). If we have chosen to live a celestial law, we will receive a celestial body, a terrestrial law, a terrestrial body, a telestial law, a telestial body. It is my understanding we will reside in that chosen kingdom forever, since there is no progressing from kingdom to kingdom after the final resurrection (see Mosiah 16:10–11). Such a plan allows God's promise of irrevocable respect for and acquiescence to an individual's agency to remain intact.

Yes, our life's longings, desires, and choices do have consequences. Since desire is a stronger emotion than longing, and if we truly become the sum of our desires, perhaps you will wish to change those lines with which we began this chapter to read:

> I *desire* to know the thoughts of God—for there is light.
> I *desire* to feel the love of God—for there is peace.
> I *desire* to hear the voice of God—for there is home.
> I *desire* to move ever Eastward.

2

DIVINE CONTRACTS

The word *covenant* means a legally binding agreement between two or more people. God established His covenant with Adam and Eve, and He has established His covenant with every generation and every living creature to come thereafter. Thus the concept of contracts with the divine is not new or novel. Covenant making is in fact central to our relationship with God.

We were all prepared from the foundation of the world to participate in the work of mortality. Our restored scriptures, coupled with the writings of prophets, describe the training Adam and Eve and other great and noble ones received before entering mortality to begin their great missions (see Abraham 3:22–28).[1] It is not unreasonable to assume each of us was similarly instructed regarding what we would encounter during our sojourn on earth. We learn that in our premortal existence we developed talents and traits that we can now call upon as we seek to fulfill our own assignments on earth. These are also referred to as *gifts,* but they are ours by right and title should we wish to claim them (see D&C 46:11–12). Why? Because we advanced in knowledge and abilities as we assisted in the work of the heavens and in preplanning and efforts to put in place all that was necessary for a mortal world.

Elder Bruce R. McConkie explains this concept: "Being subject to law, and having their agency, all the spirits of men, while yet in the Eternal Presence, developed aptitudes, talents, capacities, and abilities of every sort, kind, and degree . . . There was as great a variety and degree of talent and ability among us there as there is among us here. Some excelled in one way, others in another. . . ."[2] There we also developed a spiritual capacity, which is a type and shadow of that possessed by our heavenly parents. President Lorenzo Snow teaches: "There is the nature of deity in the composition of our spiritual organization; in our spiritual birth our Father transmitted to us the capabilities, powers and faculties which he himself possessed, as much so as the child on its mother's bosom possess, although in an undeveloped state, the faculties, powers and susceptibilities of its parents."[3]

There were no neutral spirits in the war in heaven. Every individual who has been privileged to be born on this earth agreed to the Savior's plan for mortality and actively chose righteousness and embraced the concept of agency. Having made that choice and having carefully honed spiritual and intellectual talents and abilities, we undoubtedly committed and consecrated ourselves to use those talents (gifts) in the fulfillment of our earthly missions, much as we consecrate ourselves here to use our time, talents, and energies to build the kingdom of God on earth.

There are many words used to describe this principle: *foreordination, divine assignment, personal missions.* Elder Bruce R. McConkie enlightens us: "The pre-existent life was undoubtedly an infinitely long one—of probation, progression and schooling. The spirit hosts were taught and given experiences in various administrative capacities. Some so exercised their agency and so conformed to law as to become 'noble and great'; these were foreordained before their mortal births to perform great missions for the Lord in this life."[4] Elder McConkie tells us additionally that "the mightiest and greatest spirits were foreordained to stand as prophets and spiritual leaders, giving to the people such portion of the Lord's word as was designed for the day and age involved."[5] We learn further that " . . . every person who holds the Melchizedek Priesthood was foreordained to receive that high and holy order in the pre-existent councils of eternity."[6]

President Spencer W. Kimball also asserts the truth of this: "Remember, in the world before we came here, faithful women were given certain assignments while faithful men were foreordained to certain priesthood tasks. While we do not now remember the particulars, this does not alter the glorious reality of what we once agreed to. You are accountable for those things which long ago were expected of you just as are those we sustain as prophets and apostles!"[7]

WHAT DO WE KNOW OF DIVINE CONTRACTS?

I have come to use a collective term, *divine contract,* to identify these assignments, these missions, so as not to misspeak or to presume as to the nature of the heavenly commitments at work in one's life. We know of the divine contracts entered into by some of the "great and noble ones." We know of Eve's assignment, as the mother of all living, to open the way to mortality for all waiting spirits. The scriptures teach that Abraham was foreordained to be a leader and great patriarch in God's earthly kingdom: "Abraham, thou art one of them; thou wast chosen before thou wast born" (Abraham 3:23). God told Jeremiah: "Before I formed thee in the belly I knew thee; and before thou camest forth out of the womb I sanctified thee, and I ordained thee a prophet unto the nations" (Jeremiah 1:5).

The Book of Mormon teaches us that Mary was preappointed to be the mother of the Savior, even Jesus Christ (see Mosiah 3:8). Joseph Smith was foreordained to be the prophet who would preside over the Restoration.[8] And it has been revealed that the Savior agreed long before His earthly advent to bear all our burdens and to suffer agonies unto death that He might atone for our sins, provide the resurrection, and become our redeemer and the author of our salvation (see Ether 3:14).

We know of the enormous courage and faith it took to fulfill each of these contracts. However, we have only "whisperings" of our own agreements. President James E.

Faust counsels: "Each of us . . . needs to reach down into the innermost recesses of our souls to find the divinity that is deep within us and to earnestly petition the Lord for an endowment of special wisdom and inspiration. Only when we do profoundly probe the depths of our being can we discover our true identity, our self-worth, and our purpose in life."[9]

Have you petitioned the Lord for this endowment of special wisdom and inspiration that you might know who you really are and see more clearly your purpose? Have you pled with the Lord that you might better understand your talents and abilities and how they might be combined that this life's missions might be fulfilled? Have you searched the scriptures and the words of modern-day prophets? Have you received your patriarchal blessing and if so, do you read and ponder it for insights and promises? Have you asked for strength and courage to be about your missions that all might be magnified in Christ's name?

YES, MISSIONS!

We, each of us, came to earth on a *series* of missions, not just one—but many. Some of these missions are general and are quite similar to those that will bring happiness and wholeness to all who inhabit God's kingdom, that is, family, home, and service to God, church, and community. For most others there are missions specific to themselves, based on those talents, abilities, and tendencies developed in that heavenly kingdom where we resided prior to taking up our bodies here on earth.

In a revelation to Joseph Smith we are given this assurance: "There is a time appointed for every man [and woman], according as [their] works shall be" (D&C 121:25). We are further told that if we do not live worthy to, or do not wish to complete, these missions, others will be raised to the task (see D&C 107:99–100). In God's work the principle of agency has always been at work and will always be at work, whatever our contract.

It is important to understand that a person's premortal development, assignments, and character are not necessarily to be identified by one's station in this life: "Some of the most bitter and arduous circumstances may be, in the perspective of eternity, the most blessed, and perhaps even the situations that men and women elected and agreed to enter."[10]

Though we knew we would have little recollection of the scope or of the challenges of our own personal assignments, we surely covenanted to fulfill our missions to the best of our ability. We likely recognized that one experience, one challenge, one mission would build on another and that in time we would be able to see the growth brought by these experiences, just as we see growth rings in a tree. In the end, we would see how each new experience, each new challenge, had been added to the last and how each had worked in its time to move us toward our ultimate goal of wholeness in self and in service.

Something of Our Agreements

The scriptures teach that all who have or will live upon the earth were valiant in taking care of their premortal responsibilities (see Abraham 3:26). We must have understood there what would be involved in living a rich, whole life in this sphere and what would be required of us to return as sons and daughters of the covenant. The only thing we did not fully know were the details that would make up our mortal lives.

With the light brought by Christ's restored teachings, we now can surmise that while in the premortal existence we agreed to make concern, compassion, and charity toward our fellow beings the focus of our earthly sojourn. We undoubtedly asked to be allowed, if it were within the parameters of our contract, to create a home with one we loved and to be privileged to invite waiting spirits to join us as family.

Don't you imagine that we agreed to help establish His kingdom that His truths might be available to all? We must have delighted in the knowledge that we would be privileged to participate in ordinances that would reinforce our relationship with our Heavenly Father. We would have understood that the most exalting of those ordinances would be available only in His holy temples and that the covenants made in connection with those ordinances would be binding in the heavens. We then would have agreed that all such covenants (contracts) would subject us to the laws that govern a higher state—a government headed by God the Father, His son Jesus Christ, and the Holy Ghost, and executed by the order of the Holy Melchizedek Priesthood, for that is how the whole of creation is governed.

Helps for the Journey

God has given you His own blueprint for fulfilling your missions—a blueprint that if followed, assures that your life will be filled with joyful accomplishment and safe return. This blueprint was first brought to the earth by Adam and Eve; however, many of the details of that blueprint's execution, and indeed entire sections of the print itself, were lost over time.

The plan was so vital to our purposes on earth and to our ultimate exaltation that God has sent prophets to restore knowledge of it in each dispensation of time. Then, as promised and planned in the councils of heaven, He sent His only begotten Son to deliver this blueprint anew and to perform the Atonement, which would make possible the redemption of the human race. Through His suffering, crucifixion, and subsequent resurrection, Jesus Christ became our Savior. Prior to His death, He taught the plan of salvation, gave commandments, instituted ordinances (such as the sacrament), and put in place Apostles to lead the church He thus established. Through their teachings and ministries, His gospel was to be made known to all who would listen.

As time passed, yet again, a true understanding of many of the principles, practices, and ordinances relating to the fullness of the plan was lost. Significantly, the priesthood, or the authority to administer His gospel and lead His church, was also lost. Knowing the calamity this apostasy from the truth represented, this same loving God restored through His prophet Joseph Smith, an understanding of the plan of salvation; the gospel with all its promises, ordinances, and truths; the priesthood; and the organization of His church (The Church of Jesus Christ of Latter-day Saints).

YOURS THE BLESSINGS TO CLAIM

The right to claim the blessings of this plan for the here and now and throughout all the eternities has been made available to each of us at this very moment in time because of the Restoration. This will happen as we learn and trust in its promises and power, live worthily to participate in the ordinances, and continue to make and keep covenants.

We have not been left alone to execute the details of this grand blueprint. In addition to the scriptures and ordinances and covenants, which offer the promised protection of the armor of the priesthood, we have family and friends to support us. Because we were born with the Spirit of Christ (see Moroni 7:16), we are open to inspiration and have the right, if we have been given the gift of the Holy Ghost, to claim inspired intuition. We have the life of the Savior on which to model our actions and reactions. We have a loving Father to whom we can go in prayer. We have the love, concern, and example of our leaders. We each have or can obtain a patriarchal blessing. So armed we can move forward.

DOES GOD REALLY KNOW WHO I AM?

Given the power and grandeur of God, it is often hard to comprehend how personal and intimate His relationship is with us and how personal He would like our relationship to be with Him. These verses from Psalms, with language modernized, confirm wonderful truths of this relationship:

> O Lord, you have searched me and you know me
> . . . for you created my inmost being; you knit me together in my mother's womb . . .
> My frame was *not* hidden from you when I was made in the secret place. When I was woven together in the depths of the earth, your eyes saw my unformed body.
> All the days ordained for me were written in your book before one of them came to be. (Psalm 139:13, 15–16)

We are assured earlier in that psalm that God's careful attention to us does not end when we are born into this sphere.

> You know when I sit and when I rise . . .
> You hem me in—behind and before; you have laid your hand upon me. . . .
> Where can I go from your Spirit? Where can I flee from your presence?
> If I go up to the heavens, you are there;
> If I make my bed in the depths, you are there.
> If I rise on the wings of the dawn, if I settle on the far side of the sea, even there your hand will guide me, your right hand will hold me fast. (Psalm 139:1–2, 5, 7–9)[11]

With these awesome, tender, and very personal assurances, how can we ever wonder if we are known to God, if we are alone, if He is aware of our plight, our needs, and what it will take for us to fulfill our missions?

THE LIGHT OF CHRIST

Some accept the philosophies of man as they speak of feelings and promptings. They operate on the supposition that it is chance or their own wisdom that provide the light by which they walk. They do not begin to understand the divine nature of those promptings or of that source's absolute ability to inform, direct, and guide them. Therefore the gift and the power of the gift are never claimed. That true source of which I speak is the Light of Christ.

"The Light of Christ existed in you before you were born and it will be with you every moment that you live and will not perish when the mortal part of you has turned to dust," assures President Boyd K. Packer. For many, this is important and clarifying insight. Further, President Packer informs: "Every man, woman, and child of every nation, creed, or color—everyone, no matter where they live or what they believe or what they do—has within them the imperishable Light of Christ. In this respect all men are created equally."[12]

This light of Christ is compared to the light of the sun, which is present everywhere and is given to everyone equally. When it is present, darkness dissipates—for light always has precedence over darkness. We also learn that just as the sunlight is a natural disinfectant, the Light of Christ can cleanse the spirit. This light, which comes to everyone, is bestowed in different degrees to "them that ask him according to their faith and obedience."[13]

This light, in addition to helping direct all aspects of your life, can open the door to knowledge that is already planted deep within you. Through the light of Christ, you can be given not just glimpses of information as yet unrecognized by you but occasionally pure knowledge. *This helps explain why such knowledge, when given, seems to have been always in your soul's memory bank.*

In an attempt to explain this enigma, a noted psychiatrist and author wrote of the root of the word *recognition:* "The word says we 're-know' . . . we knew it once upon a time, forgot it, but then recognized it as an old friend. It is as if all knowledge and all wisdom were contained in our minds, and when we learn 'something new' we are actually only discovering something that existed in our self all along."[14] He is speaking greater truth than perhaps he even knew.

As you seek for knowledge, as you mine the depths of materials available and the recesses of your own mind, as you study, research, ponder, and pray, doors of knowledge will be opened—inch by inch—until the light floods through unimpeded. In this manner, you can be lead to truths— pure, miraculous, essential, and ennobling.

An example of this is illustrated in a story told by James W. Cannon, professor of mathematics at Brigham Young University. He writes of his wife suggesting to him that he should pray about his research and of how he resisted doing so because he felt that part of the adventure of mathematic inquiry was discovering its secrets by and for himself.

He and his wife continued to discuss the merits of taking a prayerful approach to his work until he decided, "Well, why not?" He was working that summer on a problem he had been intermittently researching for about five years and because he lacked only one tiny insight to solve it, he determined this would be the ideal occasion to follow Alma's admonition and "experiment on my words" (Alma 32:27).

He determined to find a secluded place in the library at the beginning of each day, ponder the challenge before him, then pray for direction and enlightenment before setting out to work. "And, amazingly to me, each day I would feel instructed and directed. I would feel at day's end that I had traveled a great distance."

So went the months until at the end of the summer, as inspiration and insight had been received bit by bit, he found himself at the end of the problem. "I understood it, and the little bit of needed insight was spread over the summer and was full of miraculous mathematical wonders, much deeper than I had dreamed—and I marveled. I marveled not so much at the mathematics, because I had seen beautiful mathematics before, had occasionally had a hand in its discovery, and had even come to expect things to be richer and more beautiful than I could dream or than I could have made them had I been the creator of the universe; rather, I marveled at the naïveté that led me to expect my hard problem to have an easy answer, to assume that one little inspiration was all I needed. . . . I marveled at the distance I had traveled and at the length of my instruction."[15]

The *promise* given to Eve and to all her descendants is that the Spirit or light of Christ will ever be with us. The *plan* is that as needs arise—and as Christ is asked to be an active participant in our lives—His light will serve as instructor, guide, comforter, informer, and friend. It is my testimony that when we ask that the Light of Christ might illuminate our lives or that Christ be a full participant in solving our problems, wondrous things can happen. While this light can and will be diminished as we make choices that are morally wrong, it can never be extinguished unless we commit the unpardonable sin. That is the eternal law!

> WHEN WE ASK THAT THE LIGHT OF CHRIST MIGHT ILLUMINATE OUR LIVES, WONDROUS THINGS CAN HAPPEN.

HE HAS ARMED YOU WITH YOUR OWN "LIAHONA"

Let us consider for a moment the Liahona, that unique and useful object given to Lehi in the wilderness (see 1 Nephi 16–18). It was a compass of curious workmanship that just appeared and pointed the way that Lehi's people should go, leading them to the more fertile parts of the wilderness. It contained within it, as times warranted, writings that gave Lehi understanding of the Lord's ways. We learn that this Liahona worked according to faith and diligence, so when His children were slothful, sinful, or disobedient, it ceased to function.

We can each have such a powerful director in our lives. This spiritual Liahona is known by several names: the Holy Ghost, the Comforter, the Holy Spirit of Promise, or the Prompter. This exalted personage of spirit is in very deed the third member of the Godhead. Next to God Himself, the Holy Ghost knows more about you, your gifts, your strengths, and your weakness and how they can work together for your benefit and to the fulfilling of your divine contracts than any other.

Not an Automatic Gift

The gift of the Holy Ghost is not an automatic gift. Though he will on occasion inform or prompt anyone who inhabits the earth, the gift of his constant companionship is obtained only through faith in Jesus Christ, repentance, baptism by immersion, and the laying on of hands by His authorized servants, those who hold the Melchizedek Priesthood.

It is by virtue of our baptismal covenants that we are privileged to receive the gift of the Holy Ghost. However, we must invite him to bless and minister to us and this on condition of our worthiness. We are cautioned that this precious comforter will never labor with us if we do not live rightly, for he will not—cannot—linger in the midst of sin or indolence. Once this gift is ours and we have invited him into our lives, we will wish to so live that he can stay with us, for there is no surer guide for the journey ahead.

We are not only assured that we can have the Holy Ghost as our constant companion but that "the Comforter, which is the Holy Ghost, whom the Father will send in my name, he shall teach you all things, and bring all things to your remembrance, whatsoever I have said unto you" (John 14:26).

We are given unusual promises in this regard. We are promised enlightened minds and souls filled with joy. We are told that this prompter, when invited into our lives, will show us all things that we should do. We are promised that if we will put our trust in that Spirit which leads us to do good, to walk justly and humbly, to judge righteously, we will have light sufficient for our mortal journeys (see 2 Nephi 32:5).

The Prophet Joseph Smith taught that we can distinguish the gift of the Holy Ghost from all others, for "it will whisper peace and joy to [our] soul; it will take malice, hatred, strife and all evil from [our] hearts, and [our] whole desire will be to do good, bring forth righteousness and build up the kingdom of God."[16]

A TESTAMENT TO THE IMPORTANCE OF THE HOLY GHOST IN OUR LIVES

Joseph Smith appeared to Brigham Young in a dream or vision in 1847. When Brother Brigham inquired if the Prophet had a message for the Brethren, he was told: "Tell the people to be humble and faithful, and to be sure to keep the spirit of the Lord and it will lead them right. Be careful and not turn away the still small voice. It will teach them what to do and where to go; it will yield the fruits of the kingdom. Tell the Brethren to keep their hearts open to conviction, so that when the Holy Ghost comes to them their hearts will be ready to receive it."[17]

Elder Joseph B. Wirthlin likened this personage to the power of a light that can penetrate impenetrable darkness. He relates: "I once had the opportunity to tour a large cave. While there, the guide turned off the lights for a moment to demonstrate what it was like to be in total darkness. It was an amazing experience. I put my hand an inch from my eyes and could not see it. It was frightening in a way. I was relieved when the lights were turned back on. . . . As light penetrates the darkness and makes physical things visible, so does the Holy Ghost penetrate the spiritual darkness that surrounds us and make plainly visible spiritual things that once were hidden."[18]

As we seek to be more attuned to our life's missions, we will wish to move even closer to the sweet whisperings of the voice that is referred to by the Lord as "the unspeakable gift" (D&C 121:26; meaning glorious and great), even the Holy Comforter.

THE ELEMENT OF CHOICE AND AGENCY

A covenant with the Lord always includes the elements of choice and agency—our choice and our agency. More often than not, it is the decisions we make that determine our circumstances. We were sent to earth to do much good. Because we are human and vulnerable and have been sent here to learn, we can also make some real blunders. We can be certain that we will stumble and fall, many times over.

As we endeavor to keep our divine contracts, we may occasionally succumb to temptation, avarice, and greed. God honors His part of the contract with us even through these times. He suffers with us. He weeps for and with us. Describing the Lord's reaction to the sinfulness of man, the scriptures say: "The God of heaven looked upon the residue of the people, and he wept; and Enoch bore record of it, saying: How is it . . . that thou canst weep, seeing thou art holy, and from all eternity to all eternity?" (Moses 7:28–29).

We must never doubt that God knows us intimately and loves us absolutely. He has revealed that it is His work and glory "to bring to pass the immortality and eternal life of man" (Moses 1:39). However, He is bound by His own laws—the laws of the universe, which is just a part of the workmanship of His hands. He must let us try and fail, walk to the edge of the cliff, and if we don't listen to the promptings of the Holy Spirit, even fall off. But if we honor our covenants, He will always be there to pick us up, and He will always care about us and ensure that the Light of Christ will never entirely go out.

Life Is Meant to Be a Journey, Not a Camp

Have you noticed that life has an unsettling way of moving us about just when we think we've got it figured out?

Often the next step of the journey moves us outside the comfort zone of our familiar locales and known capabilities, sometimes at considerable discomfort or inconvenience to ourselves and others.

The Lord, who sees and knows all, allows and often inspires changes, trials, and challenges that position us to fulfill one or more of our life's missions. I have come to know that He uses the circumstances of our lives to prepare us to fulfill our divine contracts, just as I have come to know that He will use us wherever we are, if we are willing and semi-prepared to fulfill His divine purposes.

President Boyd K. Packer, speaking at a conference I once attended, related the story of his experiences in the military during World War II. He told of being at a base in Japan not long after the end of that terrible war. At that time, one was released from military service based on acquisition of points for time served, missions accomplished, and so on. By then he had accumulated more than enough points to return to home. He had been away a very long time and had seen much of war. He was weary, anxious to see his loved ones, and eager to get on with his life. Yet his commanding officer assigned him as operations officer for a search and rescue unit at Itami Air Base near Osaka, Japan.

Boyd Packer, then a lieutenant in the U.S. Air Corps, protested, pressing his righteous case to his superior officer. His plea fell on deaf ears. With no other choice, he climbed into the C-47 aircraft, grumbling bitterly over the months it would take to complete this assignment. In her book

A Watchman on the Tower, Lucile Tate quotes young Boyd: "I pled with the Lord, saying, 'Why is it?' I had never wanted anything so much as I wanted to be home. I'd prayed for it, I'd tried to earn it, I'd tried to deserve it, I'd tried to behave myself, and then, when it was within my grasp, the very thing I wanted most was denied me.

"Somehow, I don't remember how, I took hold of myself; but looking back now, I can say the Lord was answering my prayers then. There came from that experience, from things that happened in those few months, lessons essential to the preparation for the calling that is now mine. *I couldn't see that far ahead, but by those tests or trials that we receive, off-times the Lord will prepare us for what He has in mind.*"[19]

To continue the story, shortly after his arrival, young Boyd found another LDS serviceman who had begun teaching the message of the gospel to a fine citizen of that country. They often went together to teach him. Not long thereafter they were able to baptize this man, Tatsui Sato, and his son Sato. These were the first convert baptisms in Japan since 1924. Tatsui was later to translate the Book of Mormon into the Japanese language. He eventually translated other scriptures into that language as well, along with tracts, manuals, booklets, and the temple ceremony for the Laie Hawaii Temple, enabling people of Japanese descent to make their covenants in their native language. He became a great patriarch to the people of his country.

You have read President Packer's own words telling of how important this experience was in preparing him for his present mission, that of an Apostle of the Lord, a calling to which he had surely been foreordained in the premortal world. In his association with Elder Packer, Brother Tatsui was also being assisted on his own personal missions, yet specifics were not known or likely even sensed by either party at that time.

In a recent interview, Elder Russell M. Nelson recounted the time when Elder Spencer W. Kimball, then serving as an Apostle, reported to his associates in the First Presidency and Quorum of the Twelve that he had been diagnosed with serious heart problems. His doctors thought that he did not have long to live and though surgery might be performed, they did not recommend it. President Harold B. Lee advised Elder Kimball that he should do all he could to stay alive because the Lord had more work for him to do.

The story continues: "Elder Nelson, then Dr. Nelson, received a blessing from the First Presidency, saying that he had been prepared by the Lord to perform this special operation." The surgery was successfully done by Dr. Nelson. Elder Kimball, of course, lived another thirteen years and went on to become President of the Church, during which time he received the revelation that permitted all worthy males to receive the priesthood, which also opened the door for the gospel to be brought to the peoples of Africa.[20]

These examples confirm that we don't need to know the specifics of our divine contracts. We only need to open ourselves and our lives to His purposes, to consecrate ourselves to be used wherever we are and in whatever circumstances we find ourselves. The Lord will use us, and we will be stretched and in the process be further prepared for that which is ahead.

It's About Growth and Guidance

As a child I suffered from what was termed "growing pains." These pains, which attacked every joint in my body, could not be assuaged. For me, evenings seemed to be the worst time. Often my father would come and sit with me, gently massaging my knees, elbows, or arms. He would explain that in time the pains would disappear. They signified growth, and in time I would grow into my body.

Perhaps our divine contracts are a bit like that. Could they have contained within them clauses we "initialed" as to awareness and acceptance of trials and challenges necessary for growth? Could we have accepted that such growth might well stretch us to a point of real pain, with the understanding that over time and with experience we would eventually grow into our divine potential?

I suspect that there will be nothing about any of these challenges and events that will surprise us when we return home. However, for now, the really awe-inspiring challenge of mortality is that we must discover for ourselves what all this is about, what it is we have been sent here to do. The Lord, in turn, promises to give us continual guidance that will be manifested in glorious and divine ways, many of which will be recognized by us but many of which will not.

❧ 3 ❧

STRANGERS NO MORE

A most glorious truth, which should be trumpeted from the highest battlement and received with joyous shouts of hallelujah, is that each one of us comes to this earth at exactly the pre-appointed time, along with a bevy of others known to us before we were here.

They and we were sent to support one another and to help one another in the fulfillment of our missions. Elder Neal A. Maxwell speaks of this principle: "The same God that placed that star in a precise orbit millennia before it appeared over Bethlehem in celebration of the birth of the Babe has given at least equal attention to placement of each of us in precise human orbits so that we may, if we will, illuminate the landscape of individual lives, so that our light may not only lead others but warm them as well."[1] Premortal councils were not attended solely by Adam and Eve and those chosen for the highest callings; they were attended by all of us. President Joseph F. Smith shines a light into the mysteries of that heavenly world with these assurances: "We were unquestionably present in those [premortal] councils. . . . We were vitally concerned in the carrying out of these great plans and purposes; we understood them, and it was for our sakes they were decreed and are to be consummated."[2]

We are further informed that we served on committees together, accepted assignments, and, depending on need, agreed to be sent to earth at a time and place where we would be in positions to fulfill those assignments, often in tandem with those others whom we have worked beside (see Acts 17:26). Thus paths will cross and lives intertwine, bringing with that intertwining shadows of recognition, sensed, but not clearly known.

Elder Maxwell further discusses these comings and goings: "Some day, in my opinion, we shall see that these intertwinings are not simply a function of mortality but went on before in our first estate, and surely they will continue in our third and final estate! If this is true, what seem to be friendships of initiation here are actually friendships of resumption."[3] Perhaps that is why the world is filled with individuals to whom we are immediately drawn and with whom we instantly enjoy sweet association.

With knowledge of the workings of the Light of Christ, we can now understand why we sometimes recognize truths and echoes of truths in our hearts long before our conscious, mortal minds can grasp the reasons why.

Where Have I Known You?

For those of us who understand clearly the three acts of this grand drama that began in heaven, moved to earth, and which will take us finally back to heaven again, this sense of spiritual recognition should be no mystery. Yet, most of us are taken aback when we cross paths with an individual who, though unknown, seems hauntingly familiar. Do we have a longstanding agreement with them, to include them in our lives, to hold their concerns and interests as our own? Or perhaps, it is they who will hold our concerns as theirs, if only for a season, if only for a specific portion of a previously agreed to assignment.

Coincidence Is Seldom Coincidence

Elder Maxwell further teaches: "*Surprises* and *coincidences* are the words we provincial mortals often use to describe such experiences. But these are scarcely appropriate words to describe the workings of an omniscient and loving God!"[4] Let me ask you, is it a happenstance that Joseph was sold into Egypt? Or was it just by chance that Joseph Smith's parents found it necessary to move to upstate New York while he was just a boy? Or was it just coincidence that he, Neal A. Maxwell, chose not to accede to pressures and opportunities to fulfill what had been a lifelong dream of a high political career, but rather was impressed to wait upon the Lord and thus was available for assignments that prepared him to be called to serve as an Apostle of the Lord?

Everyday people experience these "coincidences" too. It seems to me now no coincidence that Betty Katana, wife of the deputy ambassador of Uganda, was so drawn to the Washington, D.C. Temple that she insisted her chauffeur find a way off the beltway to that building. Upon entering the visitors' center, she was greeted by a portrait of President Ezra Taft Benson, holding in his hand a Book of Mormon. That man, holding that same book but with its title obscured, had on at least two occasions visited her in her dreams. The earliest of those dream visitations had been when she was a young girl in her native land. The most recent time was just before she and her husband were leaving Geneva, Switzerland, to accept his assignment to the United States. In her dream, she was told that this was the book she was to take back to the children of her country.

Betty listened to all the missionary discussions and asked to be baptized within a few weeks' time. She was brought to my office at the suggestion of one of our Church leaders by another dear sister, Cleeretta Smiley. Betty's first, very impassioned inquiry was: "Why can't the Church be in my country?" She then said that she would be returning to her country within the next few days to help host an international woman's meeting. She would be staying at the home of the president of Uganda, and she thought it would be an auspicious time to introduce the gospel. Her story was so compelling that I immediately faxed all details to the appropriate General Authority with responsibilities for Africa. After prayerful consultation with others in authority, he informed me that this request seemed timely. There was a problem, however, as he was departing that evening on an international trip, and he had learned that the president of the Church's African area was also traveling. He advised that he would fax authorization for such action to the appropriate area office but asked if I, in my international capacity, might help out by contacting the member of the African Area Presidency responsible for Uganda and relaying this information and any insights I might have.

Upon inquiry, I learned that dear Elder Robert E. Sackley, with whom I had worked in Washington, D.C., was traveling in the northern part of Africa. After many telephone calls, we were able to reach him. I informed him of these developments and conveyed the message from his priesthood leader asking that Elder Sackley meet Sister Katana at the appointed time in Uganda. This was not an easy undertaking for him because travel between countries was spotty and difficult, but all was arranged. After taking a series of connecting flights, which required much of three days, he arrived to find Sister Katana at the airport. She had with her many of her friends who were waiting to be taught. The teaching went on, the land was dedicated for the preaching of the gospel, and the Church began to move forward in that country.

My Own Shadows of Recognition

In my work in international affairs for the Church from 1984 to 1997, I witnessed many situations where unlikely events or "surprise" meetings proved useful and in some cases vital to the work I was assigned to do for the Church. In sometimes exceptional ways, I met or was introduced to people of influence who had the ability and were willing to assist in opening difficult and necessary doors. It was not unusual upon meeting these people as strangers, to greet one another as friends. It is my belief that many of these "coincidences" were divinely engineered, something reinforced by a statement made by Elder Orson F. Whitney: "[God] is using not only his covenant people, but other peoples as well, to consummate a work, stupendous, magnificent, and altogether too arduous for this little handful of Saints to accomplish by and of themselves."[5]

Given what we know, isn't it likely that there were many in that grand premortal council who agreed to assist in the great work of restoring the Church in this dispensation? It has been my sense, borne out by life's experiences, that there were others whose divine contracts perhaps took them on another path, with the understanding that their help would be needed in another way as the work of the Restoration went forward.

In his excellent book entitled *The Life Before,* Brent L. Top reinforces these principles: "God designates individual spirits to come into mortality through specific nations, races, and cultures at specific times in the world's history to bring to pass his works and to fulfill his plans for all mankind."[6] Brother Top mentions a number of great spiritual leaders who have been raised up to render service and contribute enlightenment. Then he notes: "Thousands of other great and noble spirits, who were not as famous but whose service and compassion have been significant, have been and will continue to be sent to all the nations of the earth."[7]

I can attest to this truth. I have seen the work of the Church move forward on a timetable that can only be accounted for by accepting that God is micromanaging the growth and expansion of the gospel in every country, among every people. I have learned by my own experience that He has carefully placed key people in critical positions in governments, embassies, and nations to serve at the right time and in the right way—if only to perform a single task, if only for a moment. I could give you countless examples, but let me recount just two.

"Mr. Ambassador, Do You Know My Cousin?"

A number of years ago, a new ambassador from China came to Washington, D.C. Having a keen interest in that country, our Church leaders were desirous to meet him. After a period of hard work and a series of amazing "coincidences," I was able to arrange a dinner party at my home where Ambassador Zhu Quizhen and his wife met elders Neal A. Maxwell and Dallin H. Oaks of the Quorum of the Twelve. Others invited to the dinner included a number of leaders of business, industry, Congress, and the diplomatic community, along with several members of the Church and their wives. It was a wonderful evening.

After dinner a quiet meeting was convened in the

privacy of our home's library with just Elder Maxwell and Elder Oaks and the Chinese ambassador present. At that time, an invitation was extended by them to the ambassador and his wife to visit Salt Lake City as guests of the Church. While there they would meet our prophet and the other Apostles and observe something of our religion, our culture, and our people.

Arranging such an intercountry trip by an ambassador on unofficial business required extensive negotiations and serious intercultural dialogue. Eventually, the details were worked through, and the invitation was accepted. A generous CEO of a large corporation provided his private jet airplane for transportation.

Upon arrival in Salt Lake City, the diplomatic party was greeted by Church leaders, Utah's governor, and key business leaders. The ambassador gave an important speech at the Kennedy Center for International Studies at BYU. Before departing Salt Lake City on Sunday, he and his party were special guests at a Tabernacle Choir broadcast. It is the usual format of that event for the honored guest to come forward at the end of the broadcast to receive recognition and be serenaded with a special hymn. When advised of this, the ambassador said he would prefer not to step forward. Alone, Elder Maxwell went to the stand to acknowledge his presence and thank him for honoring the Church with such a visit. As Elder Maxwell turned from the podium, much to his surprise, there was the ambassador just a few steps away. He had changed his mind. After introductions and a gracious acknowledgement and thank-you by the honored guest, the choir began to sing their final song, dedicated to him. The audience was invited to join in. Much to the surprise of everyone, the ambassador sang the song with the choir and congregation. How he would know that hymn was a bit of a mystery, since he had previously indicated no knowledge of Christianity, other than intellectual, and had not expressed any familiarity with choir music, though we had discussed the Tabernacle Choir on several occasions.

A luncheon followed on the 26th floor of the Church Office Building where all could enjoy the view of the city and Temple Square. As the ambassador was escorted into the banquet room, a dear sister who was acting as a hostess approached with a scrapbook opened to a photograph of a group of university students, taken in China. Pointing to a man in the photo, she said to the ambassador, "This is my cousin's husband; do you know him?" With over a billion people in that country, what do think the likelihood would be? The ambassador graciously took the book from her hand and examined the photo. Within seconds his face was abeam with recognition. "Why, yes," he said, "that is the head of the university I attended. I valued that man."

Details were then revealed. It was a Christian university. The hostess's relative had played a key role in keeping the school open and in making learning available to those who might otherwise not have been able to get a higher education. As a young man, the ambassador had felt it a privilege to go there and had been in a choir that had sung the very hymn chosen by the Tabernacle Choir for this occasion.

This was important new information. It made it much easier for all of us to articulate to him the work of the Church and our interest in being of help in China. Because of his experience as a student, the ambassador knew the language of Christianity. He represented the nontheistic interests of his country well, but he also understood our minds and hearts and points of reference. Wherever possible he has since been an advocate and friend for the Church. Is all of that a coincidence? I think not.

At the time of this writing, there is not yet a level of religious freedom in China sufficient to allow the Church to fully function there. Attendance at public worship services is limited to expatriate members living in that country. Yet it is amazing to observe the number of outstanding Chinese people around the world who are joining the Church as they travel abroad to study or work. (The Lord certainly has His hands on that country.) There is a branch in Washington, D.C., made up almost entirely of nationalist Chinese scientists, engineers, and doctors. Many of these wonderful Latter-day Saints will perhaps return to China in the next few years. The Lord is keeping His contract, and the Church, through its educational and humanitarian arms, has been able to help that vast country in significant ways.

A Nation's Vice President and a Blessing on "All Who Will Rule Righteously"

Yes, great and good men and women have been raised around the world to play their part. There are other incredible stories to tell about the men and women of Asia, Africa, the Americas, the islands of the seas. But ultimately, it is those who have the grand apostolic callings, bearing the holy priesthood, the power to act on earth in the name of God, who can call down God's blessings on those lands by the power of that same holy priesthood.

In the spring of 1990, it seemed that there would be major changes in the philosophies and politics of those governments operating behind the Iron Curtain. Many countries were at that time throwing off the yoke of communism. New, less ideological leaders were being appointed, assigned, and elected. It seemed important that the leaders of the Church establish a rapport with the new heads of those governments, most of whom would have no familiarity at all with The Church of Jesus Christ of Latter-day Saints.

A tour of some of those countries by the Tabernacle Choir had already been planned. Was that just another "coincidence"—or was it yet another evidence that an all-knowing God had plans for these nations? After many discussions, those with responsibility for that part of the Lord's vineyard felt we could use this tour as a focus for acquainting the new leadership with concepts of religious freedom and with our church's desire to participate in that freedom. Performing its repertoire of religious and secular music, the Choir swept through Hungary, Poland, Czechoslovakia, and East Germany, thrilling audiences and making friends. They were warmly received.

Church leaders who accompanied the Choir were also received with great interest and afforded unusual respect at special dinners arranged and orchestrated by my international office and hosted by Elders Russell M. Nelson and Dallin H. Oaks in each of these nation's capitols. Contact and friendships were established with new political leaders. The goodwill generated in these events opened diplomatic channels for future access in these countries and in their embassies in Washington, D.C. With the overturn of communism, current and known ambassadors were being recalled or replaced very rapidly. We were joined at each dinner by LDS members of the worldwide business community, thus allowing these distinguished guests to come to see us more clearly as a worldwide church and religion.

There were historic happenings at each of these dinners, but I will share the details of only one, held in Russia. The Choir and its entourage arrived in what was still named the USSR on May 30, 1991. That country had not yet entirely divested itself of its communist domination or leadership. There was precious little religious freedom. The night of June 5, after the Choir's triumphant concert at the Bolshoi Theatre, our dinner was held at the beautifully restored Metropole Hotel. The dining room of this hotel is exquisite.

Gracing the enormous room with its soaring architecture were massive marble columns. The walls and the floors were marble as well. The ceiling was constructed of stained glass, and the crystal chandeliers glistened.

Because this hotel was on the same street and near the Bolshoi Theatre, there was an enormous rush into the restaurant by those invited to join us after the concert (and a number of those uninvited). All about was excitement and noise. Midway through the meal, amid the din of a hundred conversations in this room of marble, a man of obvious authority swept through the door. He was directed to me, and he asked to be taken to our hosts. I sensed that he was on a tight schedule and that he had something important to say, but I did not clearly hear his name. At that moment and by his demeanor, I wasn't certain that his presence reflected a positive turn. I took him to Elder Nelson, where the man announced that he was General Alexander Rutskoy, Vice President of Russia. He had something he wished to say to all those assembled. Barely waiting until the crowd had been quieted, Elder Nelson introduced him. Rutskoy took the microphone and by his authority of office unrolled and read a letter that proclaimed official recognition of The Church of Jesus Christ of Latter-day Saints in the entire nation of Russia. Can you imagine our joy?

The following day was a very busy one for Elder Nelson, Elder Oaks, Elder Hans Ringger (whose responsibilities as a member of the European Area presidency included the USSR) and for Gary L. Browning, president of the mission, which now included Moscow. Late in the day, they absented themselves for a brief time. As we met for dinner, I asked if I might inquire what had taken them away. Elder Nelson quietly spoke of an impression that he had, that an apostolic blessing should be pronounced on those who should rule in righteousness inside the Kremlin walls. (The country of Russia had already been dedicated for the preaching of the gospel in 1903 by Francis M. Lyman, so this was an additional blessing.)

They had hurried to the Kremlin but were too late to go inside; the gates had been closed. They went to a majestic pine tree on a hill next to the wall surrounding the Kremlin. That towering tree reached up, grew over, and cascaded down inside the wall. There, by the power of the holy priesthood, he pronounced an apostolic blessing on the peoples of that country. As a part of the blessing, Elder Nelson was prompted to invoke legions of angels to help those individuals who would rule righteously inside those walls in times of crisis.

It was some two months later that I sat with my son Tom through the night in an airport in Nairobi, waiting for a plane that didn't come until morning. Above our head on a lone television, we watched the drama play out as the president of that communist country, Mikhail Gorbachev, was detained and taken from his country house, as Boris Yeltsin took over the reins of that government, which was now to be a democracy. Central to the drama was General Rutskoy as he stood by Yeltsin's side, standing atop a military tank. Watching that incredible moment in history, we held our breaths lest Yeltsin and Rutskoy be taken captive or shot. I strained my soul's eyes to see if I could glimpse the protective "legion of angels" that had been called down by an Apostle of the Lord.

Within a short while, history was again being rewritten. Yeltsin was elected president of that newly divided republic's major country now called by its original name, Russia. However, during that short time of crisis and transition, I sensed that many divine contracts had been honored. In a nation long ruled by dictators and tyrants, that bloodless coup was surely made possible by God's Spirit moving among those people, staying hands of power that might have caused an entirely different outcome. Precious agency, so necessary if these beloved children were to fulfill their divine mission, again reigned.

WHY IS THIS IMPORTANT?

There is a plan for our lives. We can trust God. We can rely on the Savior. We can invite the Holy Ghost to be our constant companion. However, we will wish to pay close attention to the promptings of the Spirit, for it is not always easy to see God's workings in the details of our lives. Sometimes, after a season has passed and we look back, we understand that what we have been about is fulfilling one of our missions.

The important thing regarding these premortal agreements, divine assignments, or foreordinations is that we live our lives in such a way that we can be used, as needed, and as assigned, that they might be accomplished. We must open our entire souls and spirits to the possibilities; we must consecrate our lives, our time, and our talents to the Lord as willing stewards. We can thus be assured of a far more glorious journey through mortality than we could ever contemplate by ourselves.

4

THE PLAN IS CALLED "HAPPINESS"

Let us consider that plan designed by God, agreed to by two-thirds of the great council in the premortal world, and introduced to the mortal Adam and Eve as "The Great Plan of Happiness." It is a glorious, magnificent plan, designed to provide each of us with the experiences that enable us to gain needed insights, strengths, resiliency, and reliance on the Lord.

While the plan's purpose is to provide happiness and wholeness, you may be asking: "Why then is life so often fraught with trial and disappointment? Why do hard-fought-for and seemingly deserved rewards go unrealized? Why does it often seem that even the simplest dreams are unmet? *Should achieving happiness really be such hard work?*"

The short answer is "Yes." What would be the use of a life in which we are never tested, where we know no sorrow so we could never experience true joy, where we know no defeat so we can never claim victory? Is it not a wonderful paradox that our most elevating happiness comes when we have overcome the trial, survived the illness, met the test, won the battle?

The ancients believed that like heroes on a mythological journey, they were meant to struggle—to find their way through the maze, to face the dragon, and to outwit the wizard. Like heroes, they were to wrest victory out of the fiery jaws of defeat. Blessed with the light brought by Christ, we need no mythology to inform our way.

> GOD IS NOT INTERESTED IN THE POSSIBILITY OF YOUR DEFEAT. HIS PLAN FOR YOU IS VICTORY.

We have not been sent to endlessly investigate the darkness but rather to seek divine light and to walk in that resplendent light. God is not interested in the possibility of your defeat. His plan for you is victory. This requires that He deny us none of the experiences that will prepare us to return to Him in happiness and wholeness.

IT'S ABOUT FINISHING THE UNFINISHED

Elder Neal A. Maxwell advises: "The more we come to understand the plan of happiness, the more we come to understand how incomplete and unfinished we were in our first estate and how much we needed this difficult mortal experience. We finally realize that there is no other way."[1] He continues: "Remembering this reality helps, especially when the only way is so difficult and discouraging at times and when we experience sadness as participants in the great plan of happiness."[2]

There are so many caught in the abyss of challenge and discouragement. I don't have to look beyond my own street, my own congregation, to note the experience of several, as I am sure could you, not the least of which might be your own.

I know of a young couple who are caught in a sticky pit and are struggling at this very moment to find their way out. I will call them Julia and Robert. In their mid-thirties, they have lived good lives and served the Lord faithfully and well. He served a mission. Theirs is a temple marriage. They pay their tithes and offerings. They accept and perform their church callings with faith and with excellence. They have invited three lovely children into their home. Julia and Robert decided together that after they both got their degrees and were on their feet a little, hers would be the role of full-time mother and homemaker and his would be the role of full-time provider.

After working for a time in the corporate world, it seemed right for Robert to strike out on his own. Their small business was just getting off the ground when recession hit. They had extended themselves in getting into the business and extended themselves even further in purchasing a home. The investments didn't seem like that much when things were going well, but with no financial cushion and after doing all that they could, they found themselves in the position of having to sell the home they had planned for so long and sacrificed to obtain. On occasion they weren't even sure where next week's food would come from. Julia cleans houses in the morning so she can be home when the children get home from school. This is the best paying temporary job she can think of in this market at this time, though her college degree and previous work experience qualify her for much, much more. Robert at times feels near the breaking point with all the pressures, and both have shed tears, wondering why the Lord does not hear their pleas for help. Does He not care?

Now I don't know why all this has happened, but from my vantage point it appears to me that none of it is the Lord's doing. Their situation, which has become so untenable, is caused by choices, timing, and circumstances—simply the products of the world in which we live. I am, however, comfortable believing that general, if not specific, trials were discussed in the premortal world and that we understood and accepted that when we came to earth. We would not only have to endure such trials, but the experience we gained in doing so would be invaluable in our quest for eternal life. Consider the comfort the Lord offered to Joseph Smith when the Prophet cried out in despair, agonizing over the persecution and disappointment he had endured: "Know thou, my son, that all these things shall give thee experience, and shall be for thy good" (D&C 122:7).

It would make little sense to ask to come to Earth to be proven and then to ask, *"Why am I being tested?"* Elder

Richard G. Scott cautions: "Don't look for a life virtually free from discomfort, pain, pressure, challenge, or grief, for those are the tools a loving Father uses to stimulate our personal growth and understanding. As the scriptures repeatedly affirm, you will be helped as you exercise faith in Jesus Christ."[3]

The gospel assures us that God knows of our current trials and needs, and much like watching a toddler who is learning to walk, He is opening His arms and allowing us to move out on our own while yet another set of open arms is waiting to embrace us when we

It would make little sense to ask to come to earth to be proven and then to ask, "Why am I being tested?"

have taken the necessary steps. In between these two sets of open arms, He allows us the latitude necessary to try, stumble, fall, and pick ourselves up. As a toddling child, if we keep getting up when we fall down, if we keep trying, we will eventually be walking and then running without apparent effort. We will have developed the strengths and the skills necessary to take long and sure strides into the next phase of our journey.

But for now, for Robert and Julia, just getting through each day, doing everything they can to find ways to regroup and rethink career choices, trusting in friends and in the Lord seems to be all that can be done. Things will work out because of the strengths, talents, and faith of these dear people, and because the Lord will never leave their side, the

Light of Christ will ever burn in them. In the long term, they will overcome, they will be fine. But from the short-term vantage point, things look very dark just now.

The reality is there is not much to be happy about. Or is there? Their family remains together. They are all well. They haven't lost their testimonies. There are those willing to try to help. They have great abilities, which they will use to move through this part of the journey. And the Lord will keep His promises: "This too will pass." The sun will shine again. *Certainly the ending of this or any like story will depend upon how these experiences are put to use. Sometimes the greatest prize is the wisdom that is earned through faith.* With Nephi, we can say: "I know that [God] loveth his children; nevertheless, I do not know the meaning of all things" (1 Nephi 11:17). In explaining this concept, Elder Maxwell encourages us: "There have been and will be times in each of our lives when such faith must be the bottom line. We don't fully understand what is happening to us or around us, but we know that God loves us, and knowing that, for the moment, is enough."[4]

WHAT DO WE KNOW ABOUT WHAT MAKES US HAPPY?

Since this happiness, as defined in the grand plan, is the quality we are sent to find in mortality, it would be wise to delve into its workings. During the last decade, advancements in all fields of scientific research have been quite remarkable. With the development of brain imaging equipment, scientists have been able to determine which parts of the brain control certain of our emotions or responses. It seems that the "happiness center" of the brain is located in the right forward quadrant. This knowledge, coupled with research studies conducted over a long period of time, has allowed researchers to have a reasonably good idea of what happiness is *not* about and gives insight into what it *is* about. The findings reinforce what we intuitively sense. I know this may alarm some scientists, but these findings sound as though they were taken directly from the words of God and his gospel plan. Why should we find this surprising? After all, He created us, and He created us to live our lives in fulfillment of that great plan called happiness. Our brains, when studied properly, would surely reflect that.

THE THREE C'S OF HAPPINESS

The research tells us that happiness is not about money, although most assume that it is in large measure. It seems that after we have money sufficient to meet our basic needs, it doesn't make us happy; it just makes us feel that more money will make us happier. Happiness isn't found in pursuits of excessive pleasure or even in achieving fame. A relentless pursuit of activities or substances seems to magnify unhappiness rather than alleviate it. The words of Alma are well worth remembering: "Wickedness never was happiness" (Alma 41:10). Fame, unless derived from meaningful activity and worthy goals, rings very hollow indeed.

In sorting through all this research, I have concluded that there are three elements that contribute to happiness:

- Having some *control* over one's life, coupled with a sense of optimism.
- Having a belief in and a personal relationship with a Higher Being, paralleling positive relationships with at least one other human being; in other words, *connectedness.*
- Being engaged in meeting a purposeful *challenge,* that is, doing meaningful work or pursuing some satisfying activity (neither mindless drudgery nor endless play).

CONTROL

The element that comes up number one on the happiness charts is having some control over one's life. It seems that humans come "hardwired" this way. The reason for such wiring becomes apparent as we understand that this opportunity to control our behavior and therefore, to some extent, to control the outcome of our actions is key to that agency we fought for in heaven. Those who feel powerless to choose and act feel quite hopeless, a condition which is the antithesis of happiness.

Studies show that children as young as six months seem happiest, smile most often, and cry the least when they have some control over their environment. This was measured by activity that allowed these infants, by their motions, to bring images to a screen. The children quickly learned which motions made the pictures appear, and their pleasure was obvious and was so recorded. When this ability to control their environment was taken from them, they were most unhappy. Even when someone else flashed these same images on the screen for them, the infants were not content. After once knowing this control, they were unhappy when it was taken from them.

Hand in glove with the concept of control is the concept of empowerment: that permission given to us by others, or by ourselves, to act in ways we perceive as positive and to our benefit.

Central to the personalities of those who described themselves as happy was a sense of optimism and a belief in self. Without confidence in yourself, an inner belief that you can make things better or that things will work out, depression gains a foothold. This confidence—having this belief in self and in one's ability to do or act—is even more important than having specific skills, because of the attendant empowerment such belief carries with it. When life is perceived as good, it seems one can call upon hidden resources and abilities.

My father's office walls were covered with credos. As a young girl, I loved sitting on my special stool, memorizing and reflecting in my childlike way on what those "sayings" meant. One of my favorites was: "To believe yourself able has the greatest affinity to being able." I asked him over and over to explain it to me. He carefully talked me through examples of how I could call on inner resources if I would just believe they were there. If I believed I could do it, and acted as if I could do it, I would develop the skills to do what it was I wanted to do. My first experience at testing this theory came when as a young girl I accompanied him on the rounds of his rather public life. I was expected to know how to greet people and to have something to say. I was treated as an equal and was expected to behave as an appropriate companion. Though mine was a shy and very private nature, over time I was able to go out with him, meet people, act as a contributor, forget my own inadequacies, and take an interest in those we met. Over a period of years, I found that I could not only do that but that I took pleasure in these experiences. Though still of a very private nature, I have found an ability to function in the public arena because of this belief. That's what empowerment is all about. And more often than not it is the individual, rather than life, that denies his or her own abilities and therefore limits his or her happiness.

CONNECTEDNESS

The happiest people in these studies were those who had faith in a power higher than themselves. There was a real correlation between a belief in God and in expressed personal happiness. People who gleaned from such a belief a clear picture of their reason for being and who accepted the principles inherent therein as their code of conduct topped the happiness scale. These people were able to articulate the source of their happiness and to look to the future with hope, even during the bleak times. This being true, we who fully embrace the gospel and trust in and practice its principles are already several rungs up on the happiness ladder, for joy and righteousness are inseparably connected.

Elder Neal A. Maxwell advises, "One seldom-mentioned

reason for keeping the commandments is that we then become genuinely happier with ourselves. Otherwise, if unhappy with ourselves, the grim tendency is to pass our misery on, or at least to allow it to cloud and even diminish the lives of others who must put up with us."[5]

Along with a personal relationship with God, close human relationships were absolute predictors of happiness and the lack of close relationships a predictor of unhappiness. There is an intense human need to have in our lives others whom we love, others whose joys and sorrows we share and who share ours, others to touch, to hold, to hope for, and to work for. Beyond this there was a need to be engaged in active friendships, to be involved in shared projects and shared causes. Those who know but do not understand say simply, "Man is a social animal." Those who do understand know that the layers of our need run so deep and spring from a source so divine that to relegate them to mere sociability is to diminish one's nature.

CHALLENGE

And lastly, researchers found inactivity to be an absolute predictor of unhappiness. Our daily conduct must be directed to challenging, meaningful activity. Work and its attendant blessings are a gift from God. Without such activity, no matter the age, depression becomes a constant companion. With purpose-directed activity, people of all ages, from the very young to the very old, expressed about the same degree of happiness. The ideal activity provides one with a challenge, a hope for accomplishment, and a feeling of being needed.

You may be familiar with the life of the great inventor Thomas Alva Edison who worked with little rest for most of his life. In the early years, his experiments were not successful and sustenance was meager. He barely noticed, so totally absorbed was he in the challenge and in the pursuit of his dreams. His wife believed in him and did her best to keep up her part of the vineyard, scanty though the fruit. In later years, with success achieved, his wife delightedly gifted him with two weeks to go anywhere he would like in the world. He thanked her for such a lovely gift, *for making it possible for him to have two undisturbed weeks in his laboratory!*

Work does not always mean frenetic activity. Sometimes the most important work you can do is rocking a child, assisting in the search for a four-leafed clover, watching a child show off her roller blade prowess, holding the hand of a friend or of one you love, finding the beauty in the clouds of a windswept sky.

Work can also give us reprieve from other of life's refining fires. Beverly Sill, the great opera singer and later director of New York's Metropolitan Opera, spoke of the therapeutic nature of her singing. She noted that for three hours she had no troubles because she knew how it was all going to come out.

I came to know, as I worked with Ms. Sills on several occasions, something of those troubles to which she referred. This glamorous and talented woman, gifted with one of the most glorious voices of the twentieth century, had longed for children. She had looked forward to singing lullabies to them and sharing with them the joys and beauties of her world of opera. Yet one child was born deaf, the other precious child, severely retarded. Life is so often filled with such ironies.

I know women who find a similarly therapeutic outlet in their cooking, or decorating, reading, or writing. One of my friends, after fifteen-hour days, is often found, by lamplight, working in her extraordinary garden. I have a ninety-year-young sister whose hands are never idle. She finds her release in her gloriously creative knitting and crocheting, which she gives to the needy, the homeless, and the newly born.

Tied to the principle of activity is our own sense of our higher self. Our conduct needs to be in tune with our own moral code, in tune with who we believe we are at our very core. Happiness comes most often when the spirit and body are attuned. "For man is spirit. The elements are eternal, and spirit and element, inseparably connected, receive a fulness of joy" (D&C 93:33).

Living in this sphere, as eternal spirits embodied in mortal tabernacles, and possessing a gospel perspective, we have every reason to experience absolute happiness.

TRY A LITTLE LAUGHTER

We've all met individuals for whom the glass is always half empty. Many are chronic pessimists who seem to have been born that way. Such souls are not the most enjoyable to be around. Not only do they bring us down, but having a relationship with them extracts such energy that we are often left feeling drained. Our natural response is to limit or cut off contact, thus causing that individual to go into a further spiral of unhappiness. It would be nice if someone could love them enough to help them learn to use the tools of happiness.

> THE PLAN IS CALLED HAPPINESS, AND THE MORE WE KNOW OF THE PLAN, THE MORE LIKELY WE WILL ACHIEVE THAT HAPPINESS.

Research shows that one can enhance his own happiness quotient in a matter of a moment by just trying to laugh. A mirthful "aha" or a smile initiated from inside out seem to generate pleasant activity in the happiness center of the brain, as does pretending to be happy even when you aren't.

When you've laughed a bit and released yourself to fun (whether you feel like it or not), an absolute change occurs in both physical and mental responses. It seems the song "Put on a Happy Face," rather than being a hackneyed platitude, is filled with wisdom.

Looking for and grasping moments of laughter, seeking the humor in the mundane or in the crisis, can change how we deal with life and its challenges. Laughter is now believed to have a positive and curative effect on our health, certainly mental, likely physical. Most have heard the story of Norman Cousins, who believed he cured himself of what had been diagnosed as a fatal illness with laughter. He describes how this was accomplished in his book *Anatomy of an Illness*.

The plan is called Happiness, and the more we know of the plan, the more likely we will achieve that happiness that we were sent to earth to find.

5

STARRING IN YOUR OWN THREE-ACT PLAY

Most modern women's lives are filled with perplexing and often awesome ambiguities, just as was Eve's. This glorious woman who is called by the title "Eve," meaning "the mother of all living," covenanted with God to be the vessel through which waiting spirits could claim a mortal body and reside on a mortal earth. In Eden the Lord gave a commandment to Adam and Eve to multiply and replenish the earth, while at the same time commanding them not to partake of the fruit of the tree of knowledge of good and evil. Their dilemma was that they could not do both. If they were to obey the second commandment, they would not be able to fulfill the first and greater commandment. Then as the Lord has done with no other commandment, He reminded them of their agency: "Nevertheless, thou mayest choose for thyself" (Moses 3:17).

To partake or not to partake: What do we make of these conflicting commandments? Why would the Lord give two sets of instruction, both of which could not be followed? The answer is found in the most basic of our restored gospel's teachings, for in so doing God not only allowed but required a choice to be made, thereby setting into action the principle of agency in this, the second estate. Elder John A. Widtsoe helps us understand the principle at work in this seeming ambiguity:

"In life all must choose at times. Sometimes, two possibilities are good; neither is evil. Usually, however, one is of greater import than the other. When in doubt, each must choose that which concerns the good of others—the greater law—rather than that which chiefly benefits ourselves—the lesser law. . . . The greater must be chosen whether it be law or thing. That was the choice made in Eden."[1]

Choosing Between the Vital and the Merely Important

Most ambiguities arise when we are confronted with two important and good choices. It is up to us to discern those acts or actions that honor the greater law (those things that move us toward the fulfillment of our many missions) as opposed to the lesser law (those things which are secondary to that main theme and are far too often centered on self and things of the world).

To be in accord with God's intent for our lives, we must move to embrace and honor that greater law, just as did Eve. *We must learn to distinguish between those things that are vital and essential to our salvation and to that of our loved ones', as opposed to those things that are important to us and our worldly needs and expectations.*

One way to easily distinguish between the two is to understand that each of us has a mission or missions—assigned to us by God and connecting us to Him. Careers are details of larger missions and of vital importance to our mortal journeys but secondary to our first responsibility—to facilitate His work, which is "to bring to pass the immortality and eternal life of man" (Moses 1:39).

For men the ambiguities between missions and career can seem to be less pronounced. Men typically know from an early age that they will select a career that will shape their adulthood as they assume their role as breadwinner. Their education is most often directed toward degrees and career goals. Their planning likely will include serving a Church mission, having a family, and establishing a home in which they will preside. Generally, this plan includes priesthood service and community involvement, augmented by some recreational pursuits—all components of a full life lived in recognition of their life's missions.

For women it can be quite different. An attractive and obviously professional young woman posed the following dilemma at a question-and-answer period at the conclusion of a conference for single women: "I'm still confused about how I sort out the uncertainties and ambiguities of my personal and professional life. How do I go about preparing for a whole life?"

I must tell you I didn't know the full answer, nor I suspect does anyone. Finding that balance is one of the great challenges women face in mortality. I could only propose basic considerations. The answer for one woman is not the answer for another; however, there are sure principles on which to base one's choices. One important consideration is to look at your life plan in the macro rather than the micro. *Try very hard to tap into your own divine contract and always pay careful attention to where your preparation is leading you.* Is your choice or decision moving you toward fulfillment of your many missions, or is it likely to curtail your ability to complete one of those pre-appointed errands? Is your life's plan solely about career, or are you preparing for a whole life and all that such a life may require of you?

WE MUST BASE OUR LIVES ON GOD'S TRUTHS

For any life to be rich and full, it must be based on those principles that are most likely to produce happiness. Those principles are to be found in the teachings of our Savior, Jesus Christ. There is no ambiguity in them. His teachings emphasize faith, love, giving and receiving, reaching out and reaching up. The Lord teaches us to pray, to worship, to preach, to teach, to seek salvation, to accept His atonement, and to embrace both our mortality and our eternal life. His teachings are gentle and pure and filled with power and light. In our search for wholeness, purpose, and happiness, we must begin with our Savior's teachings, for God Himself has enjoined us: "This is my beloved Son, in whom I am well pleased; hear ye him" (Matthew 17:5).

The Principle of Education

One of the sure principles on which to structure a successful life in mortality, and in the eons to come, is education. Both women and men should pay close attention to educational priorities. President Hinckley counsels: "First, educate your hands and your minds. You belong to a church which espouses education." Speaking specifically to women he says: "To you young women may I suggest that you get all the education you can. Train yourselves to make a contribution to the society in which you will live. There is an essence of the divine in the improvement of the mind."[2] He then reminds us that "the glory of God is intelligence, or, in other words, light and truth" (D&C 93:36). And as a last assurance that no amount of education will be wasted he affirms "'whatever principle of intelligence we attain unto in this life, it will rise with us in the resurrection'" (D&C 130:18).

Sister Camilla Kimball, wife of President Spencer W. Kimball, said, "I would hope that every girl and woman . . . has the desire and ambition to qualify in two vocations—that of homemaking, and that of preparing to earn a living outside the home, if and when the occasion requires." Sister Kimball also pointed out that many women must support themselves because they are single, others because of illness or death of their husbands, and still others because not all of their lives are completely filled with demands of a family, home, and children.[3]

HOW DO I DIRECT MY EDUCATION?

For a woman, the question begins with what role she desires and then what role she will have the opportunity to play—and where and when. Should her education be targeted to a professional career, or should she just take a job until she marries? Supposing she never marries? At what point does she move into a full career mode? If she doesn't marry and does not make early and directed career moves, will that delay have limited her future and her security?

It would seem that so much is out of her hands. How does she know whether or not to prepare to serve a full-time mission? If she marries during college years, whose education is priority, hers or her husband's? Of course, if she marries, she'll wish to have children, but suppose her options are closed by circumstances, divorce, or death, and she must become the breadwinner? Yet, within these ambiguities, there is so much that she can control as she looks at her whole life and makes the hard decisions and the right choices that will enrich and make purposeful an entire lifetime.

WILL I NEED TO PREPARE TO PROVIDE
FOR MYSELF OR OTHERS?

Research conducted for the Church a few years ago revealed some sobering statistics about LDS women (more hopeful, but not that different from the statistics of other women). The data indicate that ninety percent of all our women will work outside the home for some portion of their lives, especially after their children are grown. More than *half* of those women will be the primary breadwinners at some time in their lives because that many will have been made single prior to reaching the age of sixty. About thirty-five percent will experience a divorce, eleven percent will be widowed, and three percent will not marry.

Faced with these sobering statistics, you should plan now for these realities because they will come whether planned for or not. Whether a young student or a mature woman, whether your education is beginning or continuing, select a field that will provide you with important and significant career skills and that will provide both a fair wage and personal satisfaction, if or when you enter the marketplace. The Lord would have you prepared to live in dignity.

Education should be ongoing, throughout an entire life, and should prepare you to enter and leave the marketplace without too great a penalty. President Gordon B. Hinckley recognizes the great challenge women face: "I would wish that all of you women might have the blessing of a happy marriage and a happy home and that you would not have to go out into the marketplace to labor for income. But I know that for some of you this may be a necessity, and you will be better equipped to do so if your hands and minds are trained."[4]

Get That Degree as Quickly as You Can

Encouragement should be given to a woman currently in school to get her degree and if time and circumstances allow, her advanced degree. She should then move into the workforce as appropriate and put those skills to the best possible uses. It would be ideal if in the process her eternal partner should come along and she is able to marry and together with her companion set priorities and plan a life that will allow her to be a full-time mother during the appropriate seasons, or all seasons if that is possible and her desire. *This choice should be recognized as a gift husband and wife give, each to the other, and not as a sacrifice on either part, although often in gifting there is something of sacrifice.* Perhaps your premortal contracts did not include marriage in this sphere. In that case, that advanced degree will become very important as you live a full, rich, and meaningful life filled with other relationships and various arenas of service.

And for those women, married, with families, who do not have the luxury of staying home fulltime, do not despair. You can be a fully committed and wonderful mother, even if you aren't able to be a full-time, stay-at-home mom. This will require serious priority-setting and deft planning. President Hinckley has said: "I recognize . . . that there are some women (it has become very many in fact) who have to work to provide for the needs of their families. To you I say, do the very best you can." With deep understanding and empathy, he advises: "I know how some of you struggle with decisions concerning this matter. I repeat, do the very best you can. You know your circumstances, and I know that you are deeply concerned for the welfare of your children."[5]

There is a celebrated passage in the chapter 31 of the

book of Proverbs, which extols a virtuous woman, characterizing her worth as "far above rubies" (v. 10). The writer goes on to say, "The heart of her husband doth safely trust in her [for] . . . she will do him good and not evil all the days of her life" (vv. 11–12). Such a woman expands her reach and "girdeth her loins with strength, and strengtheneth her arms . . . [and] she stretcheth out her hand to the poor; yea, she reacheth forth her hands to the needy. She is not afraid of the snow for her household: for all her household are clothed with scarlet" (vv. 17, 20–21). We further learn that she clothes herself beautifully, that she makes fine linens and sells them to merchants, that she is covered with strength and honor. We are also told that "she openeth her mouth with wisdom; and in her tongue is the law of kindness. She looketh well to the ways of her household, and eateth not the bread of idleness. Her children arise up, and call her blessed; her husband also, and he praiseth her" (vv. 26–28). The tribute to such a woman concludes with this counsel: "Give her of the fruit of her hands; and let her own works praise her in the gates" (v. 31). What a great model for any woman to emulate.

WORKING THROUGH THE DILEMMAS

A young woman came to me to talk about her dream of becoming a great doctor and of an opportunity that would help her realize that dream. She was at the top of her class in medical school and had been offered a scholarship and a slot in one of the most sought after programs in surgery. She was twenty-seven at that time and felt she probably would not marry and that if she did, she would likely be too old to have children. My counsel to her was based on my sense of who she was: "Continue your pursuit to be a great doctor; however, I will be surprised if you do not marry. If you do marry, I cannot imagine that you will not have children." I then asked her to answer a key question: "Is what you are planning, moving you toward fulfillment of all your missions? Will your career in surgery allow you to adapt your professional life to that of having a family?"

She later reported to me that she had taken the matter to the Lord and had listened to the prompting of the Spirit. Much to the dismay of her mentor, she had opted out of that envied surgical program. She had selected instead to specialize as a family practitioner, anticipating that would provide the flexibility that would allow her to fulfill other dreams as opportunities came along. She subsequently married, has two children, and practices medicine four days a week. She is grateful for having carefully and prayerfully thought through her options. Even so, at this point in her life, she would prefer to have more time at home with her children.

THE TWO-EDGED SWORD

For women, career choices are often two-edged swords. If you settle for less than you can be, you risk disappointing yourself and perhaps not having the wherewithal to provide for yourself and your family, should the need arise. If, however, you choose a demanding career, there may never be time enough for all you will need and want to do with your husband, children, home, church, community, and profession. There will likely never be enough of time or self to go around.

Only you can direct the acts of your play. Such direction is made easier when you truly accept your life as a series of missions, based on sacred contracts made in the long ago. Such vision gives you long-term perspective as you research and study the counsel of our prophets on this matter.

> THERE ARE WAYS,
> SEQUENTIALLY,
> TO HAVE IT ALL.

LIVING A SEQUENCED LIFE

There are ways, sequentially, to have it all. Who is not familiar with the beautiful passage from Ecclesiastes: "To every thing there is a season, and a time to every purpose under the heaven. A time to be born, and a time to die; a time to plant, and a time to pluck up that which is planted; . . . a time to weep, and a time to laugh; a time to mourn, and a time to dance; . . . a time of war, and a time of peace" (Ecclesiastes 3:1–8). But are you aware that the scripture concludes with, "I know that there is no good in them [the seasons], but for a man to rejoice, and to do good in his life" (v.12)?

Speaking at a woman's conference, President James E. Faust compared the seasons of a woman's life to the verses of a song: "It is in the soul to want to love and be loved by a good man and to be able to respond to the God-given, deepest feelings of womanhood—those of being a mother and a nurturer. Fortunately, a woman does not have to track her career like a man does. She may fit more than one career into the various seasons of her life. She cannot sing all the verses of her song at the same time."[6]

And that's what life is all about, figuring out how to determine the season you are in. Simplify and clarify the verses of your song so that as you live your life you will be ever alive to its beauty and alert to its purpose and promise and to your missions.

There Are Models to Follow

I have been fortunate to know many women who have worked through these ambiguities and found they could have it all, do it all—if they were wise enough to do it in the seasons thereof. One such woman is Ariel Bybee, formerly of the Metropolitan Opera Company, but now Artist in Residence and professor at a renowned university, where her husband heads a major department. The voice and presence of this consummate artist have always filled my heart with joy. To hear her sing "O Divine Redeemer" is to know and to worship the Savior. At my invitation, she generously and frequently came to Washington, D.C. to sing before ambassadors at our Visitors' Center Christmas Gala, in our home, and at various civic and charity events that I chaired. In this process, I have come to love her more as a sister than as a friend. Through spoken word and song, we have shared our testimonies with many sisters in gospel settings.

As we have traveled together, laughed and wept together, I have become aware of her triumphs and her struggles. I have also learned of her priorities. It became apparent that her daughter, Neylan, who could not be stronger or more delightful in all ways pleasing to the Lord, has always taken priority over Ariel's career. Next came devotion to home and Church, with years of service rendered as Relief Society president in her Manhattan Ward. Following the admonition of President Faust, Ariel Bybee has not tried to sing all the verses of her song at the same time.

Another who is more sister than friend is a great woman named Lucile Tate. You may have noticed her name as author of President Packer's biography, *Boyd K. Packer: A Watchman on the Tower.* She has written the biographies of two other Apostles, *LeGrand Richards, Beloved Apostle* and *David B. Haight: The Life Story of a Disciple,* all begun after the age of 65, the final work completed at age 81. This remarkable woman embarked on a career as her first child entered college, never imagining what the Lord had in store. She and her husband entered BYU as freshmen at the same time as did their son, the eldest of their four children. Over the next fourteen years, she and her husband and all four children had earned their college degrees.

Lucile was fifty when she received her M.A. degree and began teaching in the humanities department at Brigham Young University. Their lives went on to include a move to

Washington, D.C., a social service and a proselytizing mission, and the writing of other private and personal histories. Lucile trusted in the Lord's promise of seasons and has thus been blessed. Because of her talents as a writer and the kind of person she is, she was entrusted with that rarest of privileges, that of coming to know at such a personal level and to record for history and for posterity, the biographies of living prophets.

What About the Empty Nest?

The mission of motherhood never ceases. It is a forever tie that crosses into the eternities. But the season of day-to-day mothering eventually comes to an end. After all, that is the goal in rearing children—to send them out from Eden and set them on their own path eastward.

As the last child leaves for college, marriage, or career, days that filled themselves to overflowing abruptly become days that must be filled by you. For some women, this is no problem. They are so pleased to be able to do so many of the things they've put aside until this time that the transition is easy. For so many others, this is an extremely heart-wrenching, frustrating time. After so much nurturing, providing, and guiding, they may feel their worth has been diminished. At this point, their spouse is likely still very engrossed in his career. There are few changes in his life, and generally he is very glad about that. Men generally do not recognize that their empty-nest wife is looking for a new job description, and they will not be instinctively attuned to her needs. As a woman, it's up to you to plan for your next "growth ring," your next career, your next mission.

Recently, a husband talked to me about the problem his wife, I'll call her Norma, was having in filling her time with all the children out of the house. He was frustrated because he didn't know how to help. He simply didn't have enough emotional or physical energy to be the sole focus of her life. When Norma and I talked, she confided that she felt lonely, empty, and sad. She had waited all these years for this time when she and her husband could be together and do all the things they had put off during the children's growing-up years, and now he didn't even seem to know that she had reached a major crossroad in her life. Even more upsetting, he did not seem to want to be with her every evening but went on with his books, papers, sports programs, church assignments, and on and on. She felt as though she had lost her identity. Didn't he know she couldn't find herself? Who was she? What was she supposed to do? This was a time of enormous stress for her.

CONSIDER THE NEXT GROWTH RING

I recently heard someone say that because of changes in health and longevity, age sixty is the new fifty, and age seventy-five is the new sixty-five. If we are going to live longer and more vigorously, it is more important than ever to plan and structure the stages of our lives.

Aren't we lucky that we as women get to find new opportunities for growth and reinvent our career worlds periodically? I suggested this to Norma and also said that redefining her world wasn't something her husband could do for her. She really needed to find something she wanted to do, discuss it with him, ask for his support, and then do it.

She said that would be difficult because there wasn't anything she'd really thought seriously about doing. She had liked her life just the way it was and wasn't inclined and didn't feel qualified to start another career. Such an undertaking seemed very intimidating, and the idea of doing so took her too far out of her comfort zone. She didn't want to spend all her time volunteering. She thought about going back to school, but that seemed to require more effort than she was willing to make.

After struggling for several months, she arrived at a solution. She found a part-time job, in an atmosphere where she was comfortable, where she could train as a customer representative. Because this position required her to talk to people, think her way through situations, and choose from alternative solutions, she was using a lot of creative energy. Learning new skills and making new friends was invigorating, and in doing so she gained confidence in her own abilities and a new direction in her life's design. She also noted that by day's end she was pretty much talked and thought out and welcomed just a little companionable togetherness with her husband without having to undertake huge outings or projects.

I talked to them both a few months into this new lifestyle, and they sounded so much happier. In addition to the job, Norma had also taken up walking three miles a day and was now down to a smaller clothing size and having fun with a new wardrobe. When she factored in church and home responsibilities, life was actually *too* full again, but she liked the new vistas, and her husband liked this new, vital woman she had become.

A situation that might have led to marital strife had instead provided an opportunity for Norma to re-create herself, identify new interests and avenues of expression, and retain her pleasant partnership with her husband.

Norma had aggressively embraced the three principles of happiness: control, connectedness, and challenge, and she was now happy. A similar crisis is faced when the season is retirement. You and your husband will need to follow many of the same steps to avoid unnecessary stress in your lives.

I am not suggesting that every woman should seek employment outside the home once her children are grown. For as we have discussed, though the time spent in the role of wife, mother, grandmother, friend, counselor, homemaker, and mentor may shift, the roles never cease. What I am suggesting is that you ask yourself the right questions, put your solutions to the Lord, and follow the course that will further your life's mission.

What If You Never Marry or Are Left Alone?

The ways to achieve happiness and wholeness addressed in this book are applicable to all, single or married. However, I have been reminded by single friends of the unique challenges they face in establishing the connectedness so essential to that happiness and wholeness.

It was a valued colleague and friend who brought this forcefully to my attention. As she confided in me her feelings about never having married, I asked her at what point in her life she had realized she needed to create a whole life for herself, outside of a partnership.

She replied that she had only recently come to that realization, although she felt she had known it for some time. "For a long while I chose to run from it [creating a whole life] into comfortable, easy places, such as work, comfort food, doing things because they were expected of me—fulfilling obligations to family and friends, engaging in 'pity parties.' Now, most of those things were good, except for the pity parties and perhaps the comfort food, but certainly not all essential and definitely not all eternal."

She continued, "I now realize I chose those things rather than asking the tough questions of myself at threshold moments: 'Who am I now, what makes me happy now, what makes me feel whole now?'" Her regret: "I am now in my early fifties and just beginning to realize that I can no longer grow and progress unless I discover the answers to those questions."

ESTABLISHING AVENUES OF CONNECTEDNESS

Once you've done the hard work of identifying and honoring the person you are, there is a need to establish a lifestyle and a climate within that lifestyle where your need to be "connected" can be served.

As my colleague and I discussed that need, we compiled a list of "connectedness relationships" that will allow such needs to be met. We listed five such relationships, which are not only about people but about places.

1. **Safe havens from the storm.** It is helpful to have one or two exceptionally valued friends with whom, in a climate free from judging or judgments, you can talk about the grand and small moments of your life, let your hair down, and if need be, discuss freely your hurts and weaknesses. Such friends can be called at 3:00 A.M. for help, will take you to the hospital, bring you soup if you're sick, and even help you see the error of your ways, if necessary. These are people for whom you will do the same as needed.

2. **Relationships centering on family (your own or others).** Essential to all is a place where and a group with whom you can celebrate holidays and other moments of life worthy of special remembrance, a place where you can interact with different generations and be called into a more intimate and personal service of others, a place where you are certain to find sympathy and love, particularly when life gets overwhelming, a place where you can go to recover from illness or the slights and trials that are just too hard to bear alone. Ideally, this is your own family home, but if such is not available to you, it would be important to "adopt" a family you could serve and who would wish to include and serve you.

3. **Friends to share common causes and common interests.** How delightful it is to have friends with whom you can share dinner out, a movie, season tickets to the symphony or theater—friends with whom you are comfortable taking a little or a big trip, or who you can count on to sit by you in church or accompany you to a social event. Although such people may not be a part of your day-to-day life, it is important to develop such associations.

4. **A place where you are required to give unselfish service.** There can be no real personal and spiritual growth unless you have a relationship in which the only gifts you are expected to give are time, patience, and unconditional love and where you are required and allowed to unselfishly nurture someone. To fill this need you might become a "hugger/rocker" in a hospital for chronically ill or abandoned babies, become a Big Sister, take the kids of a too busy mother to the park and out for hamburgers on a given Saturday of each month, sit by such a mother on Sundays and help out with the kids. You might "adopt" someone living in a rest home or connect one-on-one with an elderly person in your neighborhood or church. Offer service at soup kitchens, homeless shelters, or battered-women shelters, or join a service club—the list is endless. *The need to nurture is God given and cries to be filled. The needs of others to be nurtured are similarly begging to be met.*

5. **Connectedness to the divine**. At the beginning, end, and in the center of all of this is a very personal and intimate connectedness to and absolute trust in the divine. This

personal walk with God also includes identifying with, aligning with, and fully participating in the life of His (and your) "church family." It means accepting and joyfully participating in callings, and helping plan for and attending events and celebrations of this unique family. It means testifying, sustaining, and upholding as part of the worship of your days and the trust of your nights.

As we completed this list, my friend said that this discussion had brought to mind a much earlier interview with her bishop. "I was commenting on how much I appreciated the way the ward had accepted and included me. . . . They hadn't treated me differently because I was single. . . . In other words, I felt like I belonged! In an almost immediate response he said, 'It's not the ward, it's you!' I have thought about that a lot since that meeting, and over time it has become a powerful motivator. I really am the one in control, and I really do get back what I give. If I want connection, then I must exert the effort and energy to connect."

My friend concluded our discussion by saying, "I wish I had known many years ago the importance of identifying ways and people to fill all these basic needs. My greatest disappointments and trials have come as I have tried to find or have expected to find one friend to fill them all."

Her journey has brought her to the conclusion we all, if we are lucky, will arrive at, and she expressed it in this way: "The thing that I have come to understand and for which I am most grateful is that the need for the divine connection is the most significant need in every human—and as we build that relationship, we can seek for the help needed to fill the other. That is my new journey."

THE ACTS OF OUR LIVES

Let me draw a parallel between the seasons of a woman's life and the three acts of an opera, for there are many parallels.

In opera, as in life, Act I is generally filled with light and hope, nonsense and laughter. There is growth and learning and testing, both physical and spiritual. The instincts of youth turn to love and trust. In this process, life-shaping, life-altering, life-determining decisions are made by such seemingly simple decisions as with whom and what one aligns herself, who one selects as friends, where one goes to study, and what one selects for adventure. Love is found, love is lost, and hopefully love is found again. Passion, idealism, and the need to strike out on one's quest to find one's own "holy grail" make up the components of this act of the drama.

Act II of opera, as well as of our lives, is generally the act wherein one defines one's self. As this more complete picture begins to emerge, it is shaded and highlighted by our preparation, our choices, and our actions. It is in this act that we often begin to experience the great highs and the great lows of our lives. Here one reaches out to form binding relationships. Opposites attract in life, as on stage. Partnerships are formed; but before long the concept of individuals within the partnership is lost, and we and the partner we have chosen set about fussing and adjusting and misunderstanding one another. Because of the consequences of the decisions we make in this phase of life, we often feel acted upon. We wonder why we have so little control, why we are so unsettled.

All of this is played out against a backdrop of ever-changing drama. Children are born—they grow—they struggle. Careers rise—careers fall. Loved ones die, relationships are reconfigured. By the end of this act, mature reality emerges if instead of numbly accepting the world's definition of how we should think and what we ought to be, we have clearly identified and followed our own beliefs, interests, and promptings. If we are fortunate, we will have kept the innermost soul alive and solidified our deepest and most important relationships.

The text of our lives is established by Acts I and II. Act III provides commentary on all that has gone before. At this stage, it is unlikely that we can do much to alter the larger circumstances of our lives, but we can keep adapting, changing, and growing into ourselves and our closing years. Drawing upon our experience, maturity, and acquired wisdom, we are at this point in our lives more capable of tailoring appropriate responses to new circumstances and developments. No longer driven by the passions, selfishness, and undisciplined spontaneity of youth, we can show a certain spirit—an élan—that permits us to exercise unconditional love and practice unusual generosity. We can be the grand givers, the grand mothers, and the "grand dames," witty and wise—never abashed, never unsettled. Upon turning seventy, Sister Marjorie Pay Hinckley wryly commented that she reflected repeatedly on something she had heard Stephen L Richards's wife say when Sister Richards was in her nineties: "Oh, to be seventy again! You can do anything when you are seventy."[7]

> IT IS THE THIRD ACT THAT ENDS WITH THE PHRASE, "AND THEY LIVED HAPPILY EVER AFTER."

Age can bring with it a delightful perspective. In quite another vein, entertainer Pearl Bailey said, "One has to be very old before one can learn to be amused rather than shocked." Or one can respond tongue in cheek, as did Sophie Tucker when asked about a woman's needs: "From birth to age eighteen a girl needs good parents. From eighteen to thirty-five she needs good looks. From thirty-five to fifty-five she needs a good personality. From fifty-five she needs cash."[8]

I am haunted by the words of an unknown author: "Remember, every action of our life touches some chord that will vibrate in eternity." As our seasons have been realized and utilized, we see etched in our countenances the fruits of our labors. Character replaces beauty as the lines of time defy artifice. It is at this time that the depth and breadth of the soul emerges as a Phoenix triumphant.

Ideally, it is at this stage that we become fully cognizant of the purifying power of repentance, the healing power of prayer, the sustaining power of faith, the joyous power of living in the present. It is at this time that we can look back over the whole of our lives and, if we are wise, clearly see that if any part had been missing we would not be whole. And if we've lived our lives in accordance with His will, we can conclude this act with the words of our Savior ringing in our ears: "Well done, thou good and faithful servant" (Matthew 25:21).

Our eternal lives are also played out in three acts: the first act took place in our premortal existence; the second act is played out in mortality; and the third act will see us returning home to our Father in Heaven, where we will enjoy a glorious reunion with all our loved ones who have gone before. It is the third act, we are told, that ends with the phrase, "And they lived happily ever after."

6

LET TRIALS PASS
THROUGH YOU

One of mortality's absolute certainties is that all of us will experience something of trial, disappointment, unhappiness, and pain on this earthly journey, just as all will experience times of happiness. Though life's challenges and adversities are universal, we tend to feel that they are unique to us or to our time or this generation. It is not so.

Trials began with our first parents and have not missed a generation since. Think of Adam and Eve having to endure the heartache of their son Cain slaying his brother, Abel. Imagine Mary's anguish, restrained from doing naught but to stand crushed and helpless at the foot of the cross as she witnessed the suffering of her Son, even the Savior, Jesus the Christ. Think of Emma Smith as yet another child dies, as yet another home is torched, as her beloved husband and prophet, Joseph, is martyred. Consider the suffering of the ill-fated handcart companies, whose starving members stood on frozen feet while wrapping their dead for burial. Imagine the fear of the families of 9/11, waiting amid carnage and chaos by the smoking Twin Towers for news of missing loved ones.

I've found that if you look deeply enough into any life you will find moments of not only tragedy and trials, but exquisite pain and suffering. Such suffering rubs one's soul raw; however, those who have passed through and survived this "veil of tears" are often given insights that can afford them opportunities for unusual and profound growth. These precious insights, pulled from suffering's terrible grip, can and were meant to be incorporated into a whole life and used to our advantage.

Beethoven wrote his "Ode to Joy" during the darkest period of his life. Totally deaf, and having survived a childhood of extreme cruelty, the composer drew from his anguish a sublime emotion and a soaring piece of music that reflects worshipful praise of God. Borne of sorrow and the hope of redemption, the majestic composition lifts us to unexpected heights and fills us with indescribable feelings of joy.

I recently read about Emmeline Wells, a journalist and poet of unusual abilities. Emmeline used the pages of the *Woman's Exponent,* a newspaper for Latter-day Saint women, to comfort, exhort, report, and entertain in the Church's early years. Her influence was not just local, but national and international. A brief review of a segment of her life will help to explain what forces were at work.

After her baptism in her mid-teens, she was torn from

the arms of her family by a cruel guardian who tried to keep her from her faith. Two years later, in the spring of 1844, she was on her way to Nauvoo as a young bride. "Within the next few months, the Prophet and his brother were murdered, her parents-in-law apostatized, her first child and only son died, and her husband left Nauvoo and never returned."[1]

Emmeline married Newel K. Whitney, but within five years he had died, leaving her with two young daughters. Income from teaching sustained her until she met and married Daniel H. Wells in 1852. She crossed the plains, established a home in the barren landscape of the Utah desert, and made do without much of comfort or luxury for many years, but she remained unshaken in her testimony. She bore three more daughters and spent her next twenty years in their rearing. It wasn't until 1872 that she began to write extensively. She testified that she had needed every one of her life's trials and triumphs to prepare her for her literary career.

In the farewell scene of *Anna and the King,* a movie of cinematic elegance and emotional richness, Anna poignantly says, "I have danced with a king before." Emmeline recorded in her diary a much more magnificent moment. After arriving in Nauvoo and being greeted by Joseph Smith, she recorded: "The one thought that filled my soul was, I have seen the prophet of God; he has taken me by the hand."[2]

Misery Is Optional

Elder Neal A. Maxwell wisely counsels, "Rather than simply passing through [trials], they must pass through us . . . in ways which sanctify."[3] I traveled to Canada with Rose Kennedy not long after the assassination of her second son, Robert. Having already endured the murder of another son, President John F. Kennedy, along with too many other family tragedies, she had known so much of epic sorrow in her life. Yet she seemed remarkably at peace and serenely happy, anxious to engage in all of the activities that were taking place. As we spoke of her interests, her energy, the work she had yet to do, and the power of her faith, I remarked on her amazing resilience. I shall never forget her simple response: "Birds sing after the storm, don't they?"

Another remarkable example of resiliency and wisdom is found in Helen Keller, who though blind and challenged, lived by this positive philosophy: "We could never learn to be brave or patient if there were only joy in the world."[4] The lives and outlooks of these much-admired women illustrate that our problems have only the power that we cede to them.

Brigham Young advises us that "God never bestows upon His people, or upon an individual, superior blessings without a severe trial to prove them, to prove that individual or that people, to see whether they will keep their covenants with Him and keep in remembrance what He has shown them."[5] It seems there will always be a test. We are reminded of the rainbow after the storm, the calm after the earthquake. Though we can never leave life without experiencing some measure of loss, grief, and pain, misery is optional—as is happiness. Abraham Lincoln wrote: "It is difficult to make a man miserable while he feels he is worthy of himself and claims kindred to the great God who made him."[6]

CHANGE OR CRISIS CAN OPEN THE SOUL TO THE SPIRIT

The Chinese have no written symbols for the word *crisis*. Interestingly, to express this concept you must combine two other symbols, one signifying *danger* and the other meaning *opportunity*. That is generally an accurate description of one's position as significant change enters one's life: danger plus opportunity.

It is often during these times of vulnerability or even crisis, whether of body or of soul, that we are most receptive to the tutoring of the Spirit. It follows that if we will open ourselves to and invite the Spirit in, the Holy Ghost will walk with us and dispatch unseen angels to assist and protect us, for that is his mission. Though these frightening, stressful, and anguishing experiences may be filled with unbelievable disappointment, tragedy, and pain, they needn't crush us. Rather, as we survive them, these experiences provide understanding, perspective, and strength we might not otherwise have gained. We can be victorious. It is comforting that the Lord has told us that He will give us no test, no trial, that we cannot bear (see 1 Corinthians 10:13).

Think of the words of the Lord to Joseph Smith as the Prophet was being unjustly held in Liberty Jail, under unspeakably deplorable conditions, at the whim of vile enemies: "If the heavens gather blackness, and all the elements combine to hedge up the way; and above all, if the very jaws of hell shall gape open the mouth wide after thee, know thou, my son, that all these things shall give thee experience, and shall be for thy good. . . . Thy days are known, and thy years shall not be numbered less; therefore, fear not what man can do, for God shall be with you forever and ever" (D&C 122:7, 9).

"But If Not . . . "

In a recent general conference address, Elder Dennis E. Simmons talked about having faith in the Lord Jesus Christ and maintaining an absolute commitment to His word through all our adversities. In relating the story of Shadrach, Meshach, and Abed-nego, Elder Simmons reminded us that for their refusal to worship a golden image, an infuriated King Nebuchadnezzar threatened to throw them into a fiery furnace and said: "And who is that God that shall deliver you out of my hands?" The brave, young Israelites confidently replied, "If it be so, our God whom we serve is able to deliver us from the burning fiery furnace, and he will deliver us out of thine hand, O king. *But if not,* . . . we will not serve thy gods, nor worship the golden image which thou hast set up" (Daniel 3:17–18; emphasis added). In other words, if it is not His will, for He surely has the power, they accept with absolute trust that all things will work for their good, according to the plan.

Elder Simmons concluded with these inspiring words: "We must have the same faith as Shadrach, Meshach, and Abed-nego. 'Our God will deliver us from ridicule and persecution, but if not. . . . Our God will deliver us from sickness and disease, but if not. . . . He will deliver us from loneliness, depression, or fear, but if not. . . . Our God will deliver us from threats, accusations, and insecurity, but if not. . . . He will deliver us from death or impairment of loved ones, but if not, . . . *we will trust in the Lord.*'"[7]

A WORD ABOUT CHRONIC PAIN

And to those who live in the unhappiness of chronic pain, whether of the body or the spirit, let me pass on a wonderful poem often quoted by President Spencer W. Kimball, who himself endured ever-present and excruciating physical afflictions:

> Pain stayed so long I said to him today,
> "I will not have you with me any more."
> I stamped my foot and said, "Be on your way,"
> And paused there, startled at the look he wore.
> "I, who have been your friend," he said to me,
> "I, who have been your teacher—all you know
> Of understanding love, of sympathy,
> And patience, I have taught you. Shall I go?"
> He spoke the truth, this strange unwelcome guest;
> I watched him leave, and knew that he was wise.
> He left a heart grown tender in my breast,
> He left a far, clear vision in my eyes.
> I dried my tears, and lifted up a song—
> Even for one who'd tortured me so long.[8]

Comfort can be taken from this ancient verse of scripture: "The Lord is nigh unto them that are of a broken heart; and saveth such as be of a contrite spirit. Many are the afflictions of the righteous: but the Lord delivereth him out of them all" (Psalm 34:18–19). President James E. Faust offers this helpful reminder: "When the journey becomes seemingly unbearable, we can take comfort in the words of the Lord, ' . . . I have seen thy tears: behold, I will heal thee.'" President Faust adds: "Some of the healing may take place in another world. We may never know why some things happen in this life. The reason for some of our suffering is known only to the Lord."[9] It seems the soul is like a violin string—it only makes music when it has been stretched. Perhaps joy, like grace, will come after all we can do.

There Is Much of Personal Angst Abroad in the Land

While angst is obviously not a matter for levity, Charles Schultz caught much of this unsettling anxiety that is felt by so many in one of his *Peanuts* cartoons. In the first frame, Linus is in bed, eyes raised toward the heavens. He soulfully addresses Snoopy: "Sometimes I lie awake at night and ask, 'Can my generation look to the future with hope?'" The second frame finds Linus having turned over and looking even more soulful: "Then out of the dark, a voice comes to me that says: 'Why, sure. . . . well, I mean . . . that is . . . it sort of depends . . . if . . . '"

Assurance *does* depend. It depends on so many things.

It depends on where you look for direction, hope, and solace and to whom you reach out. And it depends on who will reach out to you.

One of the major causes of this anxiety, this worry, this fear, is the social isolation that is a consequence of living in our modern world with its proliferating technology. Rather than simplifying our lives, technological advancements have made it possible for all of us to do more things at a faster pace, often without social interaction. Instead of walking down the hall to discuss a matter with a colleague at work, we now communicate through e-mails and memos. A telephone call to inquire about a matter at the bank is now answered not by a human voice but by a bevy of electronic options. We can even bypass a clerk at the grocery store and check ourselves out through an electronic scanner. With each breathless day, book-ended by too little time for what really counts and too much to do, we become more and more conflicted. Deadlines at work or in church assignments, children's needs, car pools, air travel, and meetings, limit real contact with spouse and offspring or valued friends. Young mothers, drowning in the responsibilities of caring for their children, often yearn for contact with another adult, *any* adult. The elderly are often isolated in retirement or in care centers, living without meaningful contact with family members or friends, their only companion the television or computer screen.

It is in such a climate, where no one seems to pause to touch another, that real to-the-core-of-the-soul loneliness can develop. Such loneliness cannot be ignored indefinitely, for if unaddressed it will surely lead to debilitating hopelessness. What many fail to realize is that one can be surrounded by people and yet still be alone because no one is paying attention. Elder Neal A. Maxwell attributes this to selfishness or indifference, remarking that too often "we are so busy checking on our own temperatures, we do not notice the burning fevers of others."[10]

Far too many people have to endure chronic emotional pain brought on by the above described isolation simply because they can find no one to whom they can open their hearts and no one willing to risk personal vulnerability by opening their hearts to them. Love may not solve every problem, but it can be a great healer once the roots of the problem are addressed.

Not only must we reach out, but it is important that we include enough people in our lives that they can reach out to us. When a level of trust has been established with someone we value, we need to allow them entry into our innersanctums of anxiety and stress and aloneness. It is a rare soul who can shoulder alone every human care with which he or she is burdened. A listening ear and a caring heart can be so important as one seeks, with the help of our Savior, to heal the wounds, fill the voids, and give proper perspective to the sorrows of life.

Do Not Let Such Emotions Go Untended

Psychologists tell us that living in isolation and unrelenting loneliness is very harmful. It is in such a climate that a full-fledged disease called depression takes root, for depression often finds a home when for long periods it seems nobody is really listening or when no one seems to care. Depression can rear its ugly head when every corner turned exposes a new stress, perceived or real, and when the stressed person for reasons known only to herself or himself is afraid to or unable to share these stresses with another.

Some have argued that this type of depression is genetic and that you just must accept it as another chair at the table of your life. However, a recent article published in the *Harvard Mental Health Letter* details findings that such depression is not genetically caused.[11] One is predisposed, however, to respond more negatively to stress if one's serotonin transporter gene has "short" or less efficient probes. Perhaps this is why some people seem to handle stress better than others. Perhaps this is also why the Lord invites us to turn all our troubles (stresses) over to Him and to live in the present without fear. "Draw near unto me and I will draw near unto you; seek me diligently and ye shall find me; ask, and ye shall receive; knock, and it shall be opened unto you" (D&C 88:63).

If yours is a life filled with angst or depression, reach out. Don't hide behind closed doors or closed lips. Talk, really talk, about this specific and particular concern to your spouse, to a trusted friend, to your priesthood leader, or to a qualified counselor. Most importantly, talk to the Lord and ask for promptings as to what you can do. Find ways to address this matter just as you would a broken arm or any other physical ailment.

There are other, much more serious kinds of depression caused by a chemical imbalance in the brain or spawned by terrifying experiences, sexual abuse, or other soul-scarring causes.

> *IF YOURS IS A LIFE FILLED WITH ANGST OR DEPRESSION, REACH OUT. DON'T HIDE BEHIND CLOSED DOORS OR CLOSED LIPS.*

"Dr. [Dan] Daley, who has counseled scores of [Latter-day Saints] who are coping with mental illness and depression, explained that one of the harmful myths among Church members is that, 'If I am righteous enough, I will not have depression.'"

He continues: "There are many, many righteous members of the Church who are keeping the commandments and they're doing everything right every day. They're temple-recommend worthy and they suffer from horrible, clinical, diagnosable, symptomatic depression."[12] This kind of long-lasting, clinical depression requires professional treatment if it is to be overcome. Seek medical help and stay in treatment for the long term. Enlist the help of all around you. Such depression can often be ameliorated only through treatment. But the liberating truth is that it can be treated, and life and emotions can be brought back into balance.

If yours is a simpler kind of depression, sometimes called "the blues," other remedies can put you on the path to restoration and healing. You can begin by simplifying your life and getting rid of any guilt you may be unnecessarily carrying around.

"Not My Job—Can't Fix"

Scientists have found that a woman's brain is forever processing her network of connectedness. Simply put, as a woman plans, organizes, or thinks about the present, the past, and the future, her thought process is multidimensional and inclusive. It includes both that precious circle of those for whom she *has* responsibility and others to whom she *feels* responsibility. With that perspective, she sees many things that aren't quite right, need fixing, or require adjustment. Simply put, a woman often feels she must make it all work, make all things better. That need to fix things takes enormous energy and can be intimidating and exhausting, for seldom is everything all right for everyone in the orbit of her life. When she discovers she is unable to manage or correct any or all of these conditions, she often feels inadequate or guilty, as though there is something wrong with her. This can result not only in disappointment but sometimes depression.

Think how often you feel guilty, say I'm sorry when it's not your fault, or try to fix things that have not matured to a state where they can be fixed. Wisdom dictates that everything isn't your job; you can't fix everything.

On occasion I go to an excellent acupuncturist. He is from Taiwan, his accent heavy, and his English limited. He has simplified his basic dialogue to two phrases: "My job—I fix," or "Not my job—can't fix." Women would do themselves a great service if they would look at those in their caring network and differentiate in those terms. I've even considered having cards printed with those phrases, to hand out with an appropriately checked box as needed.

It is one of the hallmarks of human maturity to be able to make these kinds of judgments—to be able to look at issues and concerns and then to wisely decide which is paramount and which we can fix.

In this matter, we might look again to Mother Eve, who when confronted with apparently conflicting commands in the garden had the courage and the ability to make the correct decision.

Be done with those nagging feelings of guilt—for not having done enough and at the right time—for all those for whom you care. Identify those feelings not as unhappiness, but for what they are: a real, holy, integral part of the grand challenges in the plan. Don't own guilt that is not yours. If it's not your job—you can't fix it.

Tie It Up—Toss It Out

Most women, whether home manager or business executive, end their days, after all are tucked in, with a few house-tidying rituals. For me they include putting the last odds and ends in the dishwasher and seeing that it is cycled, pulling the tie tight on the kitchen garbage sack and setting it by the back door for disposal, and going through the main rooms for a last-minute ordering and plumping up of the pillows.

Wouldn't we be very clever if we were to apply these same rituals to our cares and worries? We could begin by putting those odds and ends cluttering up the counters of our lives into the cleaning cycle of our minds, praying over them, and letting the Spirit swish and swoosh them about. By morning they'll be scrubbed and ready to be put into their proper place. Tie tightly the strings of the old garbage of a busy day. You've done what you could. Probably you've blundered a bit. Possibly you did at least one really dumb thing, said at least one thing you wish you could take back. But let's fix what we can and toss the rest out. Tomorrow is a new day. Then it's time to order and plump ourselves up a bit—make ourselves look, feel, and think ordered and in control, prepared to start a new day without the old baggage. It is one of the hallmarks of human maturity to be able to make these kinds of judgments—to be able to look at issues and concerns and then to wisely decide which is paramount and which we can fix. Reinhold Niebuhr's famous prayer provides useful perspective:

> God give me the serenity to accept things which
> cannot be changed;
> Give me courage to change things which must be
> changed;
> And wisdom to distinguish one from the other.

COUNTING OUR BLESSINGS

There are many reasons the gracious and generous Lord has advised us to begin and end each day with prayer. Not only does it allow us to make all our wants and wishes known, but it allows us to express gratitude, to count our blessings, and to lay our burdens on Him.

One of the blessings I count as most generous and for

which I daily express gratitude to the Lord is that awesome, restorative gift of rest. To start a new day fresh seems to me a foreshadowing of waking from our final sleep on the morning of resurrection. To count our blessings on arising into a new day does so much for our souls. Someone recently sent me such an accounting of blessing, without attribution. I found the insights so compelling that I wanted to share them.

> If you woke up this morning with more health than illness, you are more blessed than the million who won't survive the week. If you have never experienced the danger of battle, the loneliness of imprisonment, the agony of torture, or the pangs of starvation, you are ahead of twenty million people around the world. If you attend a church meeting without fear of harassment, arrest, torture, or death, you are more blessed than almost three billion people in the world. If you have food in your refrigerator, clothes on your back, a roof over your head, and a safe place to sleep, you are richer than seventy-five percent of the world. If you have money in the bank, in your wallet, and spare change in a dish someplace, you are among the top eight percent of the world's wealthy. . . . If you can read this message, you are more blessed than over two billion people in the world that cannot read anything at all.

At evening's end, after you have recounted your blessings to the Lord, you have reason to feel proud if you can say words similar to those sent in a dispatch by Vicomte Turenne to his commanding general after the Battle of Duren:

> The enemy came.
> He was beaten!
> I am tired!
> Good night.

⚛ 7 ⚛

"To Love"—Gift and Commandment

Mother Eve's absolute love for everyone waiting to claim an earthly body was manifest as a "type and shadow" of the same love that would later be shown by the Savior. This courageous woman chose to suffer physical death and the appalling possibility of spiritual death, that all who are or who have been—or who are waiting to be—might have the opportunity to experience mortality.

If we are to grasp the enormity of this act of love, we need to understand that Eve, had she so desired, could have chosen to remain ensconced in that beautiful, safe place named Eden. However, her title was Mother of All Living, and she was filled with compassion. Regardless of consequence, she chose to obey the greater law, that all might have life.

Such overriding, intervening, sacred love permeates all heavenly plans. In attempting to describe that love, Paul the Apostle taught: "Eye hath not seen, nor ear heard, neither have entered into the heart of man, the things which God hath prepared for them that love him" (1 Corinthians 2:9). Another of the Lord's early Apostles affirms: "God is love; and he that dwelleth in love dwelleth in God" (1 John 4:16). *Love, divine and directed, is not only a life force but is truly life's force.*

From Moses comes this unambiguous directive regarding love: "Thou shalt love the Lord thy God with all thine heart, and with all thy soul, and with all thy might" (Deuteronomy 6:5). This is the first and great commandment. And the second is like unto it. "Thou shalt love thy neighbour as thyself" (Leviticus 19:18). The importance of human love was reiterated by the Savior, in one of His last acts before going to Gethsemane. Said He to his Apostles: "A new commandment I give unto you, That ye love one another; as I have loved you, that ye also love one another" (John 13:34). Lest we not grasp the importance of this new commandment, hear this divine summation: "*On these two commandments hang all the law and the prophets*" (Matthew 22:40; emphasis added).

Because this concept of pure, divine, exercised love is so central to the gospel and of such vital importance to our very purpose and being, it seems wise to explore love as a gift, as a commandment, and as a very personal manifestation of who you are.

For God So Loved the World

God, of course, is the model in the ultimate act of infinite love for His children. "For God so loved the world, that he gave his only begotten Son, that whosoever believeth in him should not perish, but have everlasting life. For God sent not his Son into the world to condemn the world; but that the world through him might be saved" (John 3:16–17).

This model of love, sure and divine, is evidenced in every recorded act of the Savior's life. His teachings are centered in love, His death being the ultimate gift of love.

Lest we forget the awesome and wondrous nature of this love, as manifest by His bearing the sins of *all* humankind, let us examine for a moment what it was He suffered, first in Gethsemane and later on the cross.

The scriptures teach that Christ, as our Savior, suffered every adversity, affliction, anguish, chastening, despair, distress, misery, mockery, pain, sickness, tribulation, and trouble that had ever been or would ever be experienced by any man, woman, or child who had or ever would be born into mortality. In support of this truth, the Book of Mormon declares of Him: "He shall suffer temptations, and pain of body, hunger, thirst, and fatigue, even more than man can suffer, except it be unto death; for behold, blood cometh from every pore, so great shall be his anguish for the wickedness and the abominations of his people" (Mosiah 3:7).

That such occurred is incomprehensible in the macrocosm, but in the microcosm it becomes even more incomprehensible. Does King Benjamin mean to say that the symptoms and effects of every disease coursed through His body in Gethsemane? Did He experience every moment of grief and loss felt by every one of us at any time? Did He endure the pain, indignity, and humiliation of every sin that had ever been or would ever be committed? Did He experience the devastation of war, famine, and pestilence? Did He feel the crushed hopes of humankind and the rage and grief associated with man's inhumanity to man?

The answer to these questions is yes. And the resulting anguish was so intense that in sympathy, the very elements of the earth and the heavens went into spasms of torment. In Jerusalem "the veil of the temple was rent in twain from the top to the bottom; and the earth did quake, and the rocks rent" (Matthew 27:51). In ancient America, the devastation was even more pronounced—entire cities sank into the sea or were consumed by fire; earthquakes covered other cities with earth; tidal waves inundated the land, sweeping people and structures away; tempests and whirlwinds raged; and three days of darkness gripped the land (see 3 Nephi, chapter 10).

It is in Alma that we learn why Jesus accepted the weight of all our sins in Gethsemane and voluntarily went to his death on the cross: "And he will take upon him death, that he may loose the bands of death which bind his people; and he will take upon him their infirmities, that his bowels may be filled with mercy, according to the flesh, that he may know according to the flesh how to succor his people according to their infirmities. *Now the Spirit knoweth all things; nevertheless the Son of God suffereth according to the flesh that he might take upon him the sins of his people, that he might blot out their transgressions according to the power of his deliverance"* (Alma 7:12–13; emphasis added).

Having endured all, the Savior can and will be utterly empathetic as each of us goes through our own Gethsemane. He will cradle us; He will sit with us; and He will grieve with us. Knowing firsthand our pain and through His grace, He will forgive us of our trespasses. He will restore us, and He will redeem us. Could there be any greater act of love?

The Value, Imperative, and Importance of Love

In a letter to the Latter-day Apostles who were laboring in Great Britain, the Prophet Joseph Smith wrote: "Love is one of the chief characteristics of Deity, and ought to be manifested by those who aspire to be the sons of God. A man filled with the love of God, is not content with blessing his family alone, but ranges through the whole world, anxious to bless the whole human race."[1]

A beautiful summary of love's many elements is presented by President Gordon B. Hinckley: "Love is the very essence of life," he writes. "It is the pot of gold at the end of the rainbow. Yet it is not found only at the end of the rainbow. Love is at the beginning also, and from it springs the beauty that arches across the sky on a stormy day. Love is the security for which children weep, the yearning of youth, the adhesive that binds marriage, and the lubricant that prevents devastating friction in the home; it is the peace of old age, the sunlight of hope shining through death."[2]

The Apostle John writes: "Beloved, let us love one another: for love is of God; and every one that loveth is born of God, and knoweth God. . . . We love him, because he first loved us" (1 John 4:7, 19).

In Christ's summary of the law of love, He begins by telling us that first we must love God, and that in order to love Him it is necessary to know Him; that by knowing Him, love will follow. That same principle applies to loving our fellow humans. To love them, we must first know them and that is the fulness of the law, for "he who loveth God love his brother also" (1 John 4:21). Surely it would be out of accord with the principles of the soul to say that we love God and then not choose to love the things He loves most.

> SURELY IT WOULD BE OUT OF ACCORD WITH THE PRINCIPLES OF THE SOUL TO SAY THAT WE LOVE GOD AND THEN NOT CHOOSE TO LOVE THE THINGS HE LOVES MOST.

LOVE IS A LIFE FORCE AS WELL AS LIFE'S FORCE

Why does there seem to be such a high incidence of poverty in the world today relating to this godly concept of pure love? Perhaps it is because many feel unable to give such love and others feel unable to accept or return such love. Often it is because one person in the relationship feels unworthy of being loved. Feeling unworthy, he or she accords no respect to their finer and higher self as a literal son or daughter of God.

Another reason for not extending the love that we feel or

wish to come to feel for another is that to unselfishly extend love can be both challenging and frightening, whether it is to a partner, family member, or friend. If we are to love with a divine love, which means a love that is infinite and perfect,[3] we must open our soul to another human being and trust in that other's soul that he or she will not take lightly or betray that love. Such an outward reach requires a firm belief in self, very limited selfishness, and an extraordinary trust of another. It also requires an absolute trust in God and acceptance of the divine concept of pure love. *To truly love another, one must be willing to part with energy and emotion, to pull from the deepest places in the heart one's noblest feelings, and to unselfishly, without agenda or guile, attempt to meet another's needs.*

The teachings of the Savior and His prophets make it clear that wholeness with its subsequent happiness is inextricably linked to our capacity to extend and act on this kind of love. Indeed, "to love" is an action verb, which carries with it both command and promise.

Recognize the Wonder That Is You

Our Savior's mission was and is to teach us all we must do to return to the Father, that we may again see His face and receive through the grace of Christ the blessings of immortality and eternal life. Indeed, God tells us that His work and His glory is to bring "to pass the immortality and eternal life of man"(Moses 1:39). In case you missed it, He is talking about *you*.

Why then do so many individuals denigrate their worth? God has made it very clear that each of us is worthy of love, that to love Him we must first love ourselves, and that such love is necessary if we are to achieve what He hopes for us. He teaches that each of us is really quite "something," an unrepeatable miracle—extraordinary, unique, and individual.

We have discussed our unique relationship with God, our Father. We are known to him, every whit, just as He is known to us. Brigham Young said: "I want to tell you, each and every one of you, that you are well acquainted with God our heavenly Father, or the great Eloheim. You are all well acquainted with Him, for there is not a soul of you but what has lived in His house and dwelt with Him year after year; and yet you are seeking to become acquainted with Him, when the fact is, you have merely forgotten what you did know."[4]

So you can see we are not only the workmanship of His hand, but we came here straight from His tutoring. Never forget that He knew us before we were in our mothers' wombs, and we knew Him. He knows us by our earthly names, and He knows our talents and our abilities, which we developed as we resided with Him. I believe those abilities and talents are far more numerous than we could ever imagine.

What Is It That Makes *You* Special?

I hope you won't read further until you have taken the time to list three traits or qualities that are unique to you, characteristics that make you worthy of love. In this very minute, please pause and think of all that is wonderful about you, of all that *God* would find wondrous and wonderful about you. Record those traits in your journal or at the end of this chapter.

Now that you have done this, take time to reflect on the qualities you have listed. Next, take time to openly acknowledge these qualities and to give thanks to that God who created you and to those who nurtured and mentored you—that you might possess these traits and qualities and be the unique person that you are.

As you come to acknowledge, accept, and believe in your own worth, you'll obtain a small glimpse of that glorious person who is you and will have a greater appreciation of who you are meant to become. In this process, perhaps you will also come to feel more worthy of the love of God and more worthy of the love of others.

THE LOVING REWARDS OF FAMILY

After acknowledging the wonder that is you, move on to the wonder of the individual and specific lives that are your daily stewardship. Find ways to recognize, celebrate, and bask in the blessings of having and being part of a family. Never forget that these are the people whose names are now written into your divine contract.

Worlds are held in place by God's love. If we do not learn to love with a near perfect love here, how will we be able to hold our own worlds in place? What a blessing it is to be able to see the institution of family and the individuals therein for what they are: a gift, a privilege, a most important testing and training ground, an essential school in learning to become more like God.

I believe an agreement to love and be loved was part of the divine contract into which we entered in the premortal world. It is important, then, to shower the people we love with that same love we desire to receive. It is equally important to know that we also agreed to let others love us. So we must let them love us. These precious souls are the ones we pledged to walk in front of when they needed to be led, to walk behind when they needed to be borne up, and to walk by their side, always, that we might get one another back home again, together, just as God pledged the same to us. To this end we accepted the responsibility of becoming saviors, one to another.

Is it any wonder that the real work of perfection of self goes on within the framework of our families? Family relationships will test us in all ways. It is in these relationships that all veneer is removed and the raw stuff of which we are made shines through. It is as we learn to truly, unselfishly, and divinely love those we call family that we are able to repair, restore, and renew ourselves. It is within family relationships that we learn to curtail selfishness and hone selflessness. It is in the family that we test our capacity to love, our willingness to bear with, tutor, mentor, and adore, and temper ourselves and our desire and commitment to make sacrifices in love's name.

Indeed, the family's specific design allows the glorious privilege of experiencing a most intimate, personal, and precious love. This kind of love not only opens doors to growth but in many ways forces us to own up to our higher self and to grow in ways that can at times be quite painful as we seek to master self and our emotions. Life's unique bias is toward such growth. Such things at first glance may not seem relevant to our pursuit of eternal life, but teenage sisters learning to share a bathroom, a family coming together to provide financial assistance to a needy member, or siblings pooling their resources to provide care for aging parents all help to refine those involved and foster love for each other. Family relationships, more than any other kind, not only allow but demand that growth.

Is it any wonder that the real work of perfection of self goes on within the framework of our families? Family relationships will test us in all ways.

This life is ultimately about our safe return to our heavenly home, having learned how to love and hopefully how to love perfectly, having joined in that journey of love through binding and holy covenants with precious others. It is also about our bringing our loved ones "home" with us, "trailing clouds of glory."[5]

THE LIFE FORCE OF FRIENDSHIP

Let us marvel for a moment at the pleasures and beauty of close friendships. I know that without this special connectedness, the quotient of our joy is surely compromised and the quality of our lives diminished. Not only do friendships enhance our lives, but they play a role in how long that life will be. More than a hundred studies by social scientists show that having friends boosts the resiliency of the immune system and increases our ability to survive life-threatening illnesses. The pleasures derived from such friendships also help to improve mental health. This is reason enough to extend love to those around us.

Yet another reason to work at developing friendships is that the warmth and pleasure derived from a close relationship help insulate us from the slings and arrows of life. A true friend defends and protects us, serving as an ally and a reinforcement in the battles each of us must fight. Tellingly, as His ordeal in Gethsemane approached, the Savior seemed to take comfort in referring to His faithful followers as His *friends* (see John 15:14), and in the Prophet's time of greatest discouragement, the Lord reminded Joseph Smith: "Thy friends do stand by thee, and they shall hail thee again with warm hearts and friendly hands" (D&C 121:9).

Extending an arm of loving friendship requires the expenditure of time and emotion. That unselfish investment is what makes a cherished friendship so valuable. Because a close friendship requires reciprocity and an expectation that each is available whenever needed, perhaps not everyone who enters our lives can enjoy that special status. That's all right. Not everyone can or should be drawn into our most intimate circles. It is well to carefully select, jealously nurture, and tenderly care for our real friendships.

There is yet another dimension to relationships. They often provide spiritual awakening and growth, for they give us an opportunity to give and receive service, put someone else first, and expand our capacity to feel another's pain and rejoice in their triumphs. Knowing this, we may decide to more carefully select those people who enter and leave our circle of friends. While many may only fit into our lives as acquaintances, we need to be aware of the value of individuals and accord them the honor and courtesy they deserve as sons and daughters of God and our spiritually begotten siblings.

And finally, we need to accord positive acknowledgment to those who dwell in the outer orbit of our lives (our fellow travelers, so to speak). When we discount the worth of strangers or show intolerance or prejudice toward those we meet in our journey through life, it not only diminishes them but diminishes us. Such behavior has been shown to have a negative effect on our ability to project love and therefore causes a disruption in the balance of our souls. "The least of us, the humblest, is in partnership with the Almighty in achieving the purpose of the eternal plan of salvation. That places us in a very responsible attitude towards the human race," counsels Elder John A. Widtsoe.[6]

"Beloved, let us love one another: for love is of God; and every one that loveth is born of God, and knoweth God. He that loveth not knoweth not God; for God is love" (1 John 4:7–8).

EMBRACE THE LIGHT OF GOD IN ALL

As we come to admire and value ourselves and extend that same regard to all who are His children, we are able to see in them and in ourselves God's reflection. It is through loving others that we come to love God and enjoy basking in His light, His power, and His love. In that enhanced relationship with God, our souls will be made whole, our righteousness increased, our power magnified and multiplied. That process is how we come to be "spiritually . . . born of God" and receive "his image in [our] countenances" (Alma 5:14).

President Boyd K. Packer has said: "If we understand the reality of the Light of Christ in everyone we see and in every meeting we attend and within ourselves . . . we will have courage and inspiration beyond that which we have known heretofore. And it must be so! And it will be so!"[7]

Wouldn't it be well if you chose this day to love, to help, to forgive, to mentor, to adore, to listen to, to laugh, counsel, and cry with as necessary, all those who are part of your life's inner circle? We need to let go of the fear that blocks the love within us and prevents us from becoming God's instrument.

I've found the following three lines, committed to memory and silently repeated at times of interaction with others, have helped me:

The light of God in me embraces the light of God in
  you.
The power of God in me recognizes the power of God
  in you.
The love of God for me is perfect and infinite; I extend
  that same love to you.

A Story of Love and Healing

Let me tell you a story of love—of that kind of love. Let
me show you how a single person's love can affect lives and
how those lives can in turn affect you in very unexpected
ways. The story begins as my husband and I embarked on a
pilgrimage to a faraway nation of which we knew very little.
The year was 1986; the country was Zimbabwe. We began
our journey with broken hearts and sorrowing souls. Our
beautiful daughter, Heather, had been taken from us in an
instant. Heather, of whom one wrote, "I hurry each day to
be at my door when she passes, such is her beauty. Then I
find myself humming tunes from *Brigadoon* because I feel
such beauty could not be of this earth."

Heather lived the message conveyed in our LDS hymn
"As I Have Loved You" (no. 308). She had made the lame,
the halt, and the blind her personal concern. Additionally,
she had started a project with her father at a time of great
drought in Africa. Heather and Pierce had adopted the village of Masunda in Zimbabwe and had raised money to
build grinding mills and provide other basic necessities.
Heather's dream was to also drill a deep well so that the
people there might not suffer ever again from lack of

drinking water. After her passing, as an expression of our love for her, we pledged to make her dream come true.

With the help of family and friends, the funds were raised, and the well was completed. Pierce and I were invited to go to Masunda to dedicate it, as was the custom of the people. Wishing to see what more we could do, we arranged to make the trip. We were traveling in the north of the country when we received a call asking why we weren't at Masunda. We were advised that a ceremony, of which we were not aware as we had requested a simple, unobtrusive dedication, had been planned for the following day. With no public transportation available to us, we found a Protestant missionary plane that picked us up at a remote airstrip at sunrise and flew us to Masunda in the first light of day.

As we flew over the vast country that early morning, we were deeply impressed by its majesty and beauty. It was as though arms were reaching up to us. Approaching the area of the village, we saw people streaming from every hill into a small plain where we were to land. As we arrived, three lonely cars stood out in stark contrast to the primitive landscape. They belonged to government officials who were there for the dedication. All of the others who had gathered, numbering nearly one thousand, had made the long journey on foot.

As the festivities got under way, the leader of the people related how as the drought progressed they had been reduced to digging in the moist sand of the river bed, collecting what little moisture they could find, to save themselves, for their crops were gone. The riverbed sand was now totally dry, and they were gathered to see the end of the terrible threat to their village. A chorus of two hundred or so children sang a song they had specially written, entitled "Heather Is Life, for Water Is Life." The song depicted the idea that Heather's spirit would reside in the souls of all who drank from her well. This song, accompanied by many individual acts of love performed by the people of Masunda, in the face of such stark adversity, taught us a gentle lesson in love. We had gone there thinking we were the healers. There we were healed.

A study of the life and words of the Savior is a study of that kind of love. That is what this whole earthly test is about: to give us an opportunity to grow in love. *Christ shows us the model for love as oneness, as sacrifice, as obligation, as honor, but ultimately all of these models are individual and embrace the tremendous power our thoughts and simple acts have over circumstances and people.*

There are a thousand needs and a thousand ways to meet those needs. All of them begin and end with the word *love*. If we live with the Spirit, we won't have to think so hard with our heads. Love, without condition, will lift spirits, lighten burdens, and lead us to each other—and to God.

We must never forget that it is love that causes good to happen. Love produces peace, happiness, security, and warmth. Love is more powerful than electricity or atomic energy, more important than money. In pure love there is enough power to move mountains, to turn stony hearts to flesh, to heal and mend, elevate and inspire. Just as surely as the lack of oxygen will kill, so will lack of love. Social scientists remind us that one of the greatest gifts we can give to our immune system is a mind that thinks lovingly and faithfully. Yet love is valueless unless offered, applied, accepted, and harnessed.

We must keep our hearts open to what is possible, not what has been done. Remember the words of our hymn based on the Savior's gentle admonition with which we started:

> As I have loved you,
> Love one another.
> This new commandment:
> Love one another.
> By this shall men know
> Ye are my disciples,
> If ye have love
> One to another.[8]

ᴄ᯽ 8 ᯽ᴐ

GRASP AND GLORY IN A STATE
OF PRESENT CONSCIOUSNESS

Eve delivered a most joy-filled and joyous sermon after partaking of the fruit of mortality: "Were it not for our transgression we never should have had seed, and never should have known good and evil, and the joy of our redemption, the eternal life which God giveth unto all the obedient" (Moses 5:11). She perceived that they had chosen the better part and that it was in this life—in this present—that they would have the glorious opportunity to exercise choice, to know good and evil, to bear children, to seek redemption and eternal life.

This theme of grasping and glorying in the present is found often in the scriptures. "This is the day which the Lord hath made; we will rejoice and be glad in it " (Psalm 118:24), commands the Lord, warning us that to live according to our highest and finest design we must rejoice in a state of "present consciousnesses." The present contains within it that magical switch that illuminates, harnesses, and releases energy, light, and love, all designed to transform lives and ennoble souls.

Think about it! *It is only in the present moment that we can experience growth, listen and learn, give and receive love, exercise self-mastery, choose to do good or choose to be good.* By seizing and relishing the present, you can liberate yourself from the past and act to shape the future. Living in the present assures more richness, more abundance, more joy—right now.

VISITING THE PAST OR THE FUTURE

There are good reasons to reflect on the past or try to envision the future. Daydreams help one to visualize, to try on life scenarios, to escape for a moment into a world of possibilities, to plan. Looking to the future, planning, setting goals, and organizing thoughts are absolutely essential. *People who set no goals and have no plans or dreams accomplish little, become joyless, and prematurely grow old.*

However, living in daydreams is not the work of our lives. To be forever planning and never doing defeats all purpose of the goals we have set and the life we were sent to live. Memories help us to relive and recall those things that are too precious to forget. Indeed, events of the past should be accorded their proper honor; however, memories should be used to enrich and enliven one's life and gladden one's soul, never to provide an excuse for inaction or inactivity. New roses need to be planted daily. The past and future are prologue and epilogue; they were never meant to be the main text of our lives. Whenever the past or the future are not useful, withdraw from them and *claim* the present.

"FEAR NOT, LITTLE FLOCK"

Some of you may be saying, "All of the above sounds right, but I have so many unsettled fears and am quite unhappy. I'm just not sure I'm strong enough."

Polls taken among women indicate that far too many express unhappiness. Their reasons for such are more similar than different. They have to do with one's self, one's life, or the people in one's life never quite measuring up.

The main character in author Katherine Anne Porter's "The Cracked Looking Glass" suffers from this malady. "She sat down again with her heart just nowhere, and took up the tablecloth, but for a long time she couldn't see the stitches. She was wondering what had become of her life; every day she had thought something great was going to happen, and it was all just straying from one terrible disappointment to another. Here in the lamplight sat Dennis and the cats; beyond the darkness and snow lay Winston-Salem and New York and Boston and beyond that were far-off places full of life and gaiety she'd never seen nor even heard of. Ah, what was there to remember or look forward to?"[1]

Unfortunately, I hear such disappointment and sadness expressed by many women I meet. "What if my dreams aren't realized?" "What if I'm disappointed?" "What if I reach for something and fail?" "What if I can't forget the horrors of the past?" "What if I can't forgive those who have harmed me?" "What if someone hurts me again?" "What if I'm not smart enough, clever enough, pretty enough, rich enough, educated enough?" "What if I never marry?" "What if I never lose the weight?" "What if I agree to marry someone and someone better appears?" "What if my husband doesn't love me?" "What if my children don't measure up?" "What if my grandchildren can't find a job?" "What if we don't have enough money for our old age?"

The questions are endless, but such fears are clearly debilitating and keep us from seizing the joy that ought to be ours or experiencing the growth that is essential to our happiness. Such fear saps us of our power to act and causes us to withdraw from the present into a world filled with frightening, shadowy images that intimidate and immobilize us, destroying all sense of safety, control, and higher self. All need to know that fear is not an emotion given to us by God but by the adversary. "*For God hath not given us the spirit of fear; but of power, and of love, and of a sound mind*" (1 Timothy 1:7; emphasis added).

The specters that haunt and torment us must be pulled out into the sunlight and given names that can be understood and addressed. Consider the dark and frightening fairy tales we were told in early childhood. Though we may have cowered and shivered while imagining the dark forests, strange creatures, and evil intents of ugly people, we have long since come to see these stories for what they are—figments of imagination and not real threats to our safety and sanity. We need to make that same distinction regarding our adult fears. Rather than allowing such fears to cripple and immobilize us, we need to face and banish them. In the words of Madam Curie: "Nothing in life is to be feared. It is only to be understood."[2]

In our struggle, the Lord graciously offers us His strength and His love. "Look unto me in every thought; doubt not, fear not" (D&C 6:36), He has said. Accept the Savior's love and God's promises of this day, which He has made for you. Either God has the power to keep His promises, to renew our lives, or He doesn't. And you know that He does! Let go of fear and doubt and unhappiness. There is nothing of nobility, light, or higher self in them.

> *EITHER GOD HAS THE POWER TO KEEP HIS PROMISES, TO RENEW OUR LIVES, OR HE DOESN'T. AND YOU KNOW THAT HE DOES!*

LIVING IN A STATE OF "PRESENT CONSCIOUSNESS"

To live in a state of "present consciousness" requires that you relish, embrace, cherish, and find joy and laughter in the wonders of the world around you as well as the world inside you. How do you do this? Here are my recommendations: start with the simple things of life, for they are often the most profound. Look at, really look at, the wonder of a newborn or of a toddling child and marvel at divine design. Sit on the grass with your face upturned and feel the healing warmth of light and sun. Pluck a blade of grass, smell it, taste it. Study a butterfly. Examine a flower and count the petals. Listen to the sounds of children at play and strain to hear the laughter of that child that is still within you. Reclaim that laughter.

Look for the light in a loved one's eyes when you first come into view. Dance, really dance, to your favorite music when you're alone and you can play any role you wish. Be available to an invitation to look at the planets, see the new hummingbird nest, or observe the work of a spider making a web.

Revel in the sound and mood of this very day. Allow yourself to be stunned and drawn into the wonder of God's world as you watch the sky ablaze at sunset or rise to see a glorious dawn breaking in the eastern sky. Inhale deeply the freshness of the morning air or the sweet fragrance of approaching evening; make an outrageous wish on the first star. Rush about with kisses and hugs and ferocious declarations of affection as you say good night to all you love.

For those who are younger, I would remind you that there are few among us beyond the age of fifty who have not played the "If I had my life to live over" game. Not that we really want to go back and do it again, but because if we're lucky, time has given us perspective and insight. We do realize what should not have been missed while waiting for something else to happen and want to remind you not to miss it too.

My "do it again" list would read much like that of the late Erma Bombeck's. In a delightful column on the subject, she said that if she had her life to live over, she'd have eaten the popcorn in the good living room, invited friends over, let the wind blow in her hair, sat on the grass with the children, gone to bed when sick. "Instead of wishing away nine months of pregnancy, I'd have cherished every moment and realized that the wonderment growing inside me was my only chance in life to assist God in a miracle. . . . There would have been more I love you's, more I'm sorry's, but mostly, given another shot at life, I would seize every minute, look at it and really see it, live it, and never give it back."[3]

CHOOSE TO CREATE AND RE-CREATE IN THE PRESENT

Isn't that an interesting word? *Re-create*—to create anew. The word *recreation* thus grows from the need to fill one's cup anew. Why do so few women give themselves permission to just do things that stretch and enliven their bodies and free their minds? Men seem to be a bit more self-focused in this regard. For them a few hours spent each week to ski or to play golf or go to the gym seems a part of the natural order and generally ranks high on their list of priorities. Yet, oddly, such claiming of personal time is not often regarded by women as a necessary or essential priority. There is a very real and positive need to place priority on activities that will renew. In such a process, one is able to abandon care for a time of doing and being in the moment and emerge therefrom to greet the world with a healthier heart and fresher eyes.

Give yourself permission to re-create and then do it. Fit it into your schedule, push yourself out the door, and do it.

Perhaps it will be only a few minutes at first, but it can and should grow. If you can't find time alone, find things you can do with your children, but make it something that brings unique delight to you. The possibilities are endless and need not cost a lot of money. Join your husband or a friend for an early-morning walk. Bicycle with your kids to the library, check out a favored book, and read it under a tree in your backyard while they play. Take a yoga class, learn to make stained glass. Take up painting or learn to play a musical instrument. If you're alone, find things that bring you into contact with others—an exercise class, a walking group or book club, a dance or craft or other class, something that requires absolute commitment to the here and now. The options are endless; you fill in the blanks and be creative in the process.

Giving Myself Permission to Play

I admit, in spite of what I have said above, I still have a hard time justifying or finding time for personal recreation. I remember well one of the first times in full adulthood when I gave myself permission to seriously play. It was brought about by my adventure-loving sons. One Christmas my husband and I gave them and their wives a weeklong trip of their choosing. I anticipated they would opt for Europe, Asia, or Africa. They had in mind a scubadiving trip on a very large sailboat, which we would have all to ourselves. They had done the research to find the very best vessel and crew available. There would be a skipper and a cook and a

dive master. We would scuba dive everyday, in fact two or
three times a day, they assured. There was one major problem: I was horrified when water covered my face, even in the
shower. Needless to say, this phobia had greatly curtailed my
swimming. Actually, I could only dog paddle. How could I
ever scuba dive? "Never mind," they assured me, "we'll teach
you."

With gear in tow, we all set out to take a series of lessons
that would certify us as dive qualified. I will not chronicle
the nightmare those lessons were for me. Suffice it to say that
by the time I received my certification, I had fractured two
ribs as a result of vigorously throwing up underwater. The
reason I saw it through was more centered in self than in
bravery. I just couldn't imagine spending seven days in the
middle of the ocean with nothing to do. Besides, I didn't
want to miss out on any of the fun.

The sailboat was all that it was advertised to be, the climate divine, the sky cloudless. And then that first real dive
in those pristine, aqua-colored waters. What an incredible
world we discovered. Never have I seen such beauty or
known such peaceful serenity. By the end of our adventure,
I was the one who wanted to stay down the longest and dive
the deepest. I returned home restored, refreshed, re-created.

Some years later, as we sat together on the beach at
Belize at the conclusion of a family dive vacation, I thought
of the joy I had found in sharing this activity with my
family, of the closeness it had brought, and of the pleasure I
personally had found. I wondered why I had waited till the

half-century mark to discover how exhilarating this particular kind of stretching and growing could be. As I pondered this I realized what it was: it had taken me that long to release myself from my image as one who always had to be doing, working, creating, providing, taking care of someone else's needs.

At that same time, I released my physical self. It was all right if my figure wasn't quite that good in a swimsuit; it was all right if my hair was bleached by salt water; it was all right if my makeup washed off. As I thought of all the things I had not done because of those kinds of concerns, I was overcome with a sense of waste. But I also thought how nice it was to have arrived at that point.

That trip was a once-in-a-lifetime experience. But the activity doesn't always have to be that exotic. We can find a similar sense of adventure closer to home, in our own backyards or communities. And to re-create doesn't always need to be about physical activity. One can give time at a soup kitchen, do family history research, visit children or grandchildren, or plan a party for the neighborhood children. Re-creating is about giving yourself time and space from the routine.

GO OUT AND JUST HAMMER

There are many novel ways to re-create. I love doing things with my hands—big things, such as making cornices and covering furniture. I also love just putting things together, whether it be assembling an object or putting together a beautiful room. I love designing and building houses—everything about the process, from drawing the plans to the smell of freshly cut boards and the elegant, bare-bones, open-to-the-sky structural framing. I love going to concerts in the park, or concerts anywhere, and having serendipitous days, where in the process of being out and about wonderful things just occur. Life is so multi-dimensional. How can we ever get it all in?

My husband built a workbench in the garage for my needs. There I just make things and then create designs on them. Sometimes they work, sometimes they don't, but with music filling the space and a stipple or other brush in one hand and a hammer or glue gun—or whatever—in the other, I have fun seeing what I can make that's beautiful out of something that's just around. After an hour or so, I'm ready for the next "stuff" that life requires of me. I'm not an artist. I just do what pleases me during this time. And during this time, I operate under this motto: "Some things worth doing are worth doing poorly." For me, it's about creativity and release; it's not about perfection.

Learning to Live, Really Live

As you learn to relish the present and come to see each day as a fragile, perishable gift from God, the present will be drawn into sharper focus, and you will live with greater intensity and a greater sense of thanksgiving. You will love more and more deeply, you will become alive to the possibilities. You will rejoice and be glad in it.

Another important part of living in the present is that you simplify your life, your activities, your needs, in such a way that the present affords peace, serenity, and pleasure. We all have too many things that demand lodging, care, cleaning, attention. If something isn't giving back to me, I have finally learned to remove it from my life. It's taken me a very long time, but at last I have learned to live more simply, eat more simply, dress more simply. This doesn't mean that you give up style, elegance, fine dining, joyous entertaining—or whatever pleases you. It does demand that you get rid of all that excess that demands that you care for it, clean it, organize it, put it away, and then use it so you won't feel guilty.

Accept yourself; find joy in the simple things that make up the routine of your life. Declare that happiness to the Lord at the end of each day. It does no good to focus on what you have lost. Good only can come from concentrating on what you have left at this very moment. Sadness, fear, and guilt are harmful; they will immobilize you and use energy you cannot spare. Vision is limited and divinely so. We don't get to choose how we'll die, only how we'll live. Try, really try, to recognize each new dawning, each arising, each minute of the present as an unrepeatable miracle; seize it, embrace it, partner with God in the living of it, joyously, freely, and without fear.

9

CREATING AND RESIDING IN SPACES MADE SACRED

I began this book by speaking of our longing for our heavenly home, yet such longing is not limited to our yearning for heavenly spheres. *Hearth* and *home* are those words here on earth, next to *God, mother, father,* and *children,* which generate the most warmth in our hearts—and, when one is away from home, the most longing in our bosoms.

Return once again with me to Eden, the place where our journey began. A careful reading of the scriptures reveals that by choosing to partake of the fruit of the tree of knowledge of good and evil, our first parents became mortal and capable of having children. Thus began the cycle of birth and death that makes it possible for the spiritual offspring of God to be clothed in mortal bodies, live for a season on the earth, be tested, die, be resurrected, and then return to their heavenly home. In the inspired document "The Family: A Proclamation to the World," the leaders of The Church of Jesus Christ of Latter-day Saints have declared without equivocation: "The family is central to the Creator's plan for the eternal destiny of His children." We also learn that "the family is ordained of God" and that "marriage between man and woman is essential to His eternal plan." It follows that the home is vitally important, indeed, a sacred institution.[1]

Clearly, the home is intended to be more than just a shelter from the elements or a place of protection and love, although it should be all of that. A home is to be, in addition, a place where children are nurtured and where intellectual and spiritual learning takes place.

That is the kind of home Adam and Eve provided for their children: "And Adam and Eve blessed the name of God, and they made all things known unto their sons and their daughters" (Moses 5:12). We see this model of home as a place wherein the stories, records, and legends of families are held precious and passed from generation to generation, a place where all things of God and His works are made known. Our homes are intended to be a model of heaven—celestial workshops, so to speak.

During His mortal sojourn, Jesus sought out just such homes—places marked by peace and solace, welcome and shelter, friendship and kinship. It is in these homes that He received His disciples, washed their feet and they washed His. It is there that He supped, blessed the inhabitants, and taught His disciples and others the gospel of love and salvation.

After His resurrection, Jesus visited the people of the new world—His "other sheep," whom He had promised would also hear His voice (see John 10:16). During a day of teachings, framed in language so sublime and filled with truths so powerful that they could not be described, the Lord said to His listeners: "I perceive that ye are weak [tired], that ye cannot understand all my words which I am commanded of the Father to speak unto you at this time. Therefore, go ye unto your *homes,* and ponder upon the things which I have said, and ask of the Father, in my name, that ye may understand and prepare your minds for the morrow, and I come unto you again" (3 Nephi 17:2–3; emphasis added). One must believe that those homes were likewise places of refuge, prayer, learning, and love. Following this model, we can establish our own homes in keeping with the divine purposes that have been outlined here.

HOW DOES A HOME WORK BEST?

As discussed, first and foremost our homes should be a place of shelter and peace, a fortress of strength, a place of light amid an ever darkening world. Following the same pattern established by the Lord for His own house, we should make our homes sacred by ensuring that they are also "a house of prayer, a house of fasting, a house of faith, a house of learning, a house of glory, a house of order, a house of God" (D&C 109:8). President Harold B. Lee spoke to this point when he asked: "Where is the first line of defense in this church? Is it the Primary? Is it the Sunday School? That is not the way our Heavenly Father has revealed it. . . . You will find that the Lord placed squarely on the forefront of the battlefields against the powers which would break down these defenses, the home, the first line of defense. (See D&C 68:25–32.)"[2]

A home, by its very nature and highest use, will be filled with the hustle and bustle of living, but its atmosphere can and should be Spirit filled and hallowed. All who reside under its roof should feel and should consider that Spirit. Remember, it is not the grandeur or the furnishings of a home that make it holy; it is what happens in that home. Upon opening the door, one should hear "sounds pleasing unto the Lord," whether it be sounds of laughter, sounds of shared conversation and play, sounds of music that is pleasing to the ear and whose lyrics present positive sentiments, for those lyrics will stay in the memory long after the music is silenced. It may be something as simple as the ordinary but comforting sounds of pots rattling in the kitchen, a child practicing the piano, or a ball bouncing off the basketball standard in the driveway.

WARMTH AND WELCOME

If our homes are to be a safe haven, when that home's inhabitants enter, there should be at least one who steps forward and expresses delight at their return. How delightful if the first gesture upon entry is a loving arm around the shoulder, a whispered "I love you," or a shoulder-squaring grasp of loving hands and a voice that affirms, "I'm really glad you're here; tell me all the good things that happened to you today, and if bad things happened, let me hear about them and comfort you." There will always be an eagerness to return to such a home. In such an atmosphere, the Spirit will feel welcome and will linger. When no one is physically at home to extend a welcome, a note of greeting left on the counter, food available in the refrigerator, a light that has thoughtfully been left on, all speak of warmth, love, and concern. Children should be taught to welcome each other back into the home with pleasantness and civility as well.

Since yours is to be a house of prayer, regular family prayer should be a part of the routine of your home. Sister Marjorie Pay Hinckley reminds us: "It is good to kneel as a family and to hear daily expressions of gratitude to our Heavenly Father for the blessings we enjoy. The Lord intended His children to enjoy the good things of life. With all that we have, we must also have grateful hearts. We must teach our children not to take all that they have for granted. . . . Never let a day go by without saying thank you to some-one for something—and especially to your Heavenly Father."[3]

There are other ways to invite the Spirit into our homes and to call upon the Lord for blessings that are precious and will be held precious by those residing therein. Father's bless-ings; father/mother report/counseling sessions; family home evenings; great stories; projects undertaken together and talked about with pleasure; traditions designed, honored, and followed; a yearly blessing on the home and the inhabi-tants therein—each and all of these will add to a home's holiness. Recently, I heard someone say: "We have a right to angels standing guard over our children and our homes." Every parent should lay claim to that right.

A Home of Peace and Preparation

On our way home from a trip to Africa, my husband and I accepted an invitation to stay in such a home with a precious couple and their young family. This family resided in the residence of the American embassy in Stockholm,

> We have a right to angels standing guard over our children and our homes.

Sweden. Greg Newell was, at that time, the youngest ambassador to represent our country. With his beautiful wife, Candilyn, and their five children, one born after their arrival in that country, the Newells had taken the country by storm.

Their vitality, talents and abilities, graciousness, and family togetherness had all become legend.

However, our reason for wanting to be with them for a long weekend was to see that all was well with them. We had embraced them as a part of our family from their early days in Washington, D.C. We needed to feel the spirit of their home away from home. From welcome to departure that spirit was magnificent. It was clear amid all the activity that theirs was a house of order, a house of prayer, a house of learning.

On Sunday morning, we awakened to the sounds of Tabernacle Choir music playing in the family quarters and quiet and beautiful preparations for Sabbath worship underway. That should have been no great surprise, but it would have been so easy for it to have been otherwise. The days before Sunday had been crammed with events and activities. Saturday night had witnessed a very large and elegant dinner party in our honor, attended by a significant bevy of foreign diplomats. As it was the habit of that household to show a family's welcome to all, the children had stayed up to greet and entertain the guests prior to dinner. It would have been so easy for Greg and Candi to have slept in a bit on Sunday and to let the children run about. But this was not the nature of that home. I learned an important lesson from this great couple and this great family. Their orientation was clear. It was eastward, and it has continued ever since in that direction.

CHECKING ON YOUR FAMILY'S ORIENTATION

Knowing what we know about our premortal life, don't you suppose that when we came to earth and asked to be allowed to invite precious spirits into our home, we also promised to keep a very close eye on the orientation of those little ones? We must have understood it would be our responsibility to do for our children as the Lord did for Adam and Eve when He inquired of them, "Where goest thou?" To ask that question and feel confident you have ascertained the truth is easier when your charges are all in your home and you can not only see them clearly but can converse often, give them a father's blessing, sit on their bedside, chat upon their return from activities, hear their prayers, and turn the lights out after all are safely tucked in.

However, when your children are grown and have established families of their own, often living thousands of miles away, it is harder to share the wonder that is their growth, to see how their joys and sorrows, trials and challenges are shaping their souls, though you speak together often and visit regularly. Certainly, we have found this to be the case as our sons have married, moved away, and begun having children of their own. Our interest in knowing the desires of their hearts remains undimmed.

We had an opportunity recently to share some of these deepest insights. A major wedding anniversary was approaching for Pierce and me. Throughout the previous year, we received, generally through our daughters-in-law (isn't it the nature of women to keep the activities going?) innocent inquiries as to lists of names and addresses of friends, veiled references to a big event, and so on. Now, this anniversary was a most significant landmark, and we did wish to celebrate—but the desire of our hearts was for a quiet celebration with our children. Therefore, we sent a letter to our sons, a part of which follows:

"You have asked us what it is we would like for our wedding anniversary. Thank you for caring. This is a milestone that is worthy of pause, remembrance, and celebration.

"You have quietly offered parties, sought address lists of our friends with an eye to requesting letters of memories from them and so much more. While each idea has merit, this is not where we are in our lives. Our time with friends has been spectacular; however, with reflection we can readily recall those times. Parties are always great fun, but we've had more than our share of those with friends, with the greats and near greats of the world, with those who are only acquaintances. What we long for, what we never have enough of, is time with family.

"We want to know your hearts, to share more of your memories, your hopes, and your dreams. To this end we would be delighted if on this anniversary, you would compile a book that would contain your memories of times and events in your lives; wives and children are not exempt. In addition to anything you would like to put into this book, we would request three photos of each of you (not more— not less) that identify times and places unique to you. Most importantly, we would like you to include a letter that would articulate answers to the following questions—with examples, please, and we would like, if possible, these books and letters to be presented and read to us in person."

The list of questions read as follows:[4]

- The seven defining moments of your life (It goes with-out saying that the highest order of defining moments are when you meet and when you marry the person of your dreams and each time a precious child is born— so we ask you to go beyond these to the next level.)
- The six most interesting things you've done
- The five pivotal people in your life
- The four greatest spiritual "aha's" of your life

- The three things you would be unwilling to live without
- The two achievements of which you are most proud
- The one word you would like spoken as a statement of you

We simplified this list of requests for those under twenty. However, even the youngest, our then-nine-year-old granddaughter Heather, completed this assignment with great finesse, and we saw into the real person she is and learned things about her that we had not suspected.

Our two sons and their wives flew in to spend two days with us. What a feast of sharing that was. That evening, after eating dinner at our favorite restaurant, we hurried home, and until the wee hours of the morning, we read our letters aloud. Amid laughter and tears, testimony, and side trips down memory's lane, we learned not only what their orientation was at that juncture of their lives but also the events that had shaped them. Many of the things they shared with us had not previously been articulated, and Pierce and I came to appreciate a side of our adult children we had not known. We loved and valued all that was revealed. Our children asked that we answer the same questions and present our replies as well. Both we and they learned much not previously known, even after decades of togetherness. This defining, clear sense of direction was important to the here and now and will be to the future.

A wonderful model of family gathering and ongoing teaching and counseling has been preserved for us: "Three years previous to the death of Adam, he called . . . the residue of his posterity who were righteous, into the valley of Adam-ondi-Ahman, and there bestowed upon them his last blessing. . . . And Adam stood up in the amid of the congregation; and, notwithstanding he was bowed down with age, being full of the Holy Ghost, predicted whatsoever should befall his posterity unto the latest generation" (D&C 107:53, 56).

YOUR CHAPEL AS YOUR SANCTUARY

One day some years ago, I was in my office in Washington, D.C., when I received a telephone call from a prominent Jewish rabbi. We had served together on a national interfaith organization and had come to know and admire one another. After greetings he asked if I was aware of an event called *Kristallnacht* ("the night of the broken glass") that had occurred in Germany prior to the start of World War II. I said I had heard of it but that I would like to hear the story from his lips.

He told me that on the nights of November 10 and 11 of 1936, uprisings had occurred throughout Germany against the Jewish people. On those two nights, thousands of Jewish establishments, including synagogues, businesses, and homes, were ransacked and ravaged. In towns large and small throughout Germany, mobs raged, smashing windowpanes and as many chandeliers and lights as could be accessed in order that the hated Jews would be left in darkness. Many Jewish people were killed or injured as they tried to protect their property. The frightening events of that night were the beginning of the Nazi Party's evil design to solve the "Jewish problem," and that initial violence led to horrors beyond belief, which are now known collectively as the Holocaust.

My rabbi friend continued: "We feel it is time for a symbolic gesture of healing, unity, and reconciliation—to turn the lights back on, so to speak. Therefore we are asking churches throughout America to leave their lights on in their sanctuaries throughout the night. Will you ask the leadership of your church if they will participate?"

I was taken aback to be reminded of those terrible atrocities and told him that even though the time was short (the designated night was just ten days away), I would pass his request on at the highest levels. I expressed my hope that the leaders of the Church would agree to participate in the symbolic gesture and help facilitate the binding of wounds.

As I hung up the phone, I thought, *Of course, he means that place inside our meeting houses where we worship and take the sacrament.* I had not previously thought of our LDS chapels as sanctuaries, although that is the term used by most religions to describe the holiest place inside their buildings or cathedrals. I knew also that historically the sanctuary of a church had been considered sacrosanct. From ancient times, there had been nearly universal agreement that if a fleeing person could somehow get inside a church, his enemies were obliged to leave him be. The sanctuary was considered holy, inviolable, and a safe haven, and even the most corrupt armies, police, or governments generally abided by this convention.

I spent some time then and have often since pondered the word *sanctuary*—a place of refuge, asylum, shelter, safety. I have thought of the many things that occur in our chapels that provide sanctuary. It is there that we partake of the sacrament and are thus reminded of the debt of gratitude we owe the Savior. In that sacred ordinance, we partake of bread and water in remembrance of His love, His suffering, and His triumph over sin and death. As we partake of the simple elements, we renew the covenant we made with Him when we were baptized, promising always to remember Him and to keep His commandments. In return for our obedience, He promises that we will always have His Spirit to be with us, providing us sanctuary against temptation and sin.

It is in the sanctuary of the chapel that we listen to, learn about, and ponder the words of eternal life and find in them incentive to avoid the evils of this world. It is there that we bask weekly in our fellowship with the Saints, drawing strength from one another and pledging mutual support. In our chapels, our children find sanctuary from the temptations that surround them, as they associate with others of like values and like interests, while learning the truths that will help them safely through their journey.

Next time you enter your chapel, think of all the things that occur therein that make it a sanctuary, sacred to you and yours. Declare these thoughts and that sacredness to your children. Ponder these ideas as you enter and as you take the sacrament. Speak about these feelings over Sunday dinner and at other quiet and personal times. Teach your children to reverence both the edifice and the sanctuary to be found therein.

The greatest of all earthly sanctuaries are our holy temples. Temples, by their design, purpose, and dedication are areas of sacred space made holy because God's presence can be found there. Each time one enters the temple, one is in essence entering Eden, for there, as in Eden, we are in a place wherein God can dwell, wherein we can make holy covenants and learn all things necessary to enable us to pass the sentinels and angels who guard the way that leads (eastward) back into the presence of God.[5] Elder M. Russell Ballard reminds us: "There is a spirit in the house of the Lord that exists nowhere else in the world. Those who worthily enter the temple to worship and to serve are invited to partake of a spiritual feast that provides sustenance for starving souls."[6] Live each day that you may partake of this feast. Go often to sup.

NATURE AS AN AREA OF HALLOWED SPACE

The noted naturalist John Muir said, "When we try to pick out anything by itself, we find it hitched to everything else in the Universe."[7] I think of a description of mountains as templed hills pressing their faces up to God. I think of special glades and groves wherein God has made Himself, His son, the Godhead, and His purposes known to mortal men. I think of the crystal streams of my youth swirling down canyon rocks, pristine lakes shimmering in the sunlight, shadowed trails, high mountain meadows carpeted with morning flowers. As I stand in these places, I hear remnants of songs, based on scripture, playing on my memory's stereo: "Rivers crawl to find Him, mountains move—just to let Him through."[8]

Nature provides havens of light, places you can and should share with those most precious to you and where you can go to meditate, commune, or just quietly "be." Put to such use, these beautiful settings become sacred space wherein we can see the handiwork and grandeur of God. Elder Ballard also encourages us in this regard: "Think of what would happen if all of us took time to appreciate the wonders of nature that surround us and to give thanks to the Creator of this beautiful world."[9]

Stuart Kind, the author of the stirring hymn "How Great Thou Art," expressed for all of us the wonder of the Lord's creations:

> When thru the woods and forest glades I wander,
> And hear the birds sing sweetly in the trees,
> When I look down from lofty mountain grandeur
> And hear the brook and feel the gentle breeze,
> Then sings my soul, my Savior God, to thee,
> How great thou art! How great thou art![10]

Get out and commune. Walk in gardens and groves, amid mountains and streams. Take those you love with you.

Time spent in family or mother/daughter–father/son excursions can do much to build relationships and bond souls. Or go alone for a day of solitary contemplation, searching, and healing. I know of those who have found answers to life's problems by being in the stillness of nature and communing with God, whether in a sheltered garden in the midst of city traffic, or shaded glade miles from the nearest human. These are often the settings wherein we can best hold still our souls and listen, really listen, for answers to our prayers.

CREATE YOUR OWN "ARKS OF REMEMBRANCE"

Specially created or crafted boxes set aside to house the documents and mementoes heralding the high moments of your life can become sacred space to you and yours. Perhaps this will be where you will place the original copy of your patriarchal blessing, certificates of ordination, your baptism certificate, your marriage license, souvenirs of special events, awards, medals, certificates of merit, special photographs, a child's drawings.

Such mementoes have value beyond the things they document. They are tangible evidence also of the things you cherish most in life, a testament of what is important to you. I recommend that each child in the family be provided their own special repository. Often I give a box of fine wood, beautifully crafted and appropriately engraved, as a wedding present with a suggestion that the bride and groom put it to such use in conserving their own treasures.

At the time of the death of a beloved mother of five

young children, I presented a remembrance box to that dear husband and his children with a suggestion that those things the children would most like to share with their mother be placed therein. I felt sure she would know of the box and take pride in what was inside. The father subsequently told me how special the box had become to the children as each deposited there the things that their mother would have enjoyed seeing—school papers, printed programs and mementoes of special events, ribbons and awards, certificates, and photographs taken of family gatherings. He also said that it was not unusual to see a child going through the items in the box as they were putting inside something precious of theirs.

Space is sacred and has power, just as does time. Accord each its proper respect.

ᴄ⤳ 10 ⤳

Claim the Dialogue— Claim the Gifts

The name *Adam* as used in the Garden of Eden was plural and meant both Adam and Eve. There God walked and talked with both of them, that His words, guidance, and love might benefit them equally. The same principle holds today. Unless a dialogue or address at general conference, sacrament meeting or other venue, or a communiqué in a book, periodical, or other medium says that a message is specific to one group, all messages are meant for women as as well as for men. Unless used specifically, the word *man* as used in the scriptures and by the Brethren means both men and women. That we might not misunderstand, the Lord revealed to Joseph Smith, "[God] created man, male and female, after his own image and in his own likeness" (D&C 20:18).

A few years ago, a woman asked me why the Brethren seldom address women directly and specifically in their general conference speeches. I pointed out the scripture cited above, which indicates that when it appears in the scriptures, the word *man* refers to both *man* and *woman*. I also said that it was my testimony that in our search for answers to gospel questions or for comfort or counsel that would answer our personal needs, all messages from the pulpit or written messages from the General Authorities apply equally to men and women. When the Savior directed Peter and the other Apostles to "feed my sheep" (John 21:16), isn't it apparent he meant *all* His sheep—man, woman, child, saint, sinner, blind, or whole? All messages relating to the restored gospel are Christ-centered and are intended to further the grand work of helping us successfully negotiate the perils of this life—keeping us correctly oriented and on the path that will ultimately lead us "home," clothed with immortality and eternal life, successful participants in the great plan of happiness. Could there be any among us to whom these messages do not apply?

Nonetheless, during the next general conference, I decided I would pay particular attention to exclusive references to women.[1] The list I made ended up being two pages long and included such phrases as "daughters of God and of the covenant." Women were referred to as "elect ladies," and specific instructions were given to us to be anxiously engaged in testifying, unifying, teaching, accepting challenges, finding strength in prayer, offering charity, being a righteous partner, supporting the priesthood, heeding the prophet, creating righteous families, and protecting those families with shields of faith. Clearly, the Brethren were equally concerned with the roles of men and women, and I found in their messages a joyous affirmation of womanhood. As I reflected on all that had been directed to women and with President Gordon B. Hinckley's reminder given in that conference that "this is the season to be strong," I penned the following verses :

Do divine assignments whisper to you,
Evoking memories of what's yours to do?
Who you are and are to become!
Eternal designs—decrees—welcomed.
Holy daughters of the covenant,
'Tis your season to be strong!

Yours to testify steadfast in Christ—
Unifying, teaching, seeking the light,
Challenge accepted—strength in prayer.
Evincing charity, compassion, care.
Courageous daughters of the covenant.
Joyous reasons to be strong!

Called to be sister, partner and Saint.
"Woman of God," heart never faint.
Priesthood supported—prophets to heed.
Willing to follow, ready to lead.
Beloved daughters of the covenant.
Ever needed to be strong!

Assigned and accepted that noblest of roles:
Creator and keeper of precious souls.
Teaching the gospel—a shield of faith.
Covering, protecting, keeping safe,
Trusted daughters of the covenant,
Blessed reason to be strong.

Claim, then, promises of power and depth.
Sacred oaths pledged and kept.
Queens, priestesses, kingdoms, thrones.
Joyous reunions, eternal homes!
Glorious daughters of the covenant.
This is your season to be strong.

Laying Claim to Gifts of the Spirit

There are great gifts that come directly from God to women and that women have every right to claim. The Apostle Paul discusses the availability of such gifts: "To one is given by the Spirit the word of wisdom; to another the word of knowledge . . . to another faith . . . to another the gifts of healing" (1 Corinthians 12:8–9). Additional great and glorious gifts are enumerated, all of which are given by the Spirit. Latter-day revelation confirms: "For there are many gifts, and to every man is given a gift by the Spirit of God" (D&C 46:11).

> There are great gifts that come directly from God to women, which they have every right to claim.

Throughout the centuries and down to modern days, many good and righteous men have felt comfortable in claiming these gifts, while too often equally good and righteous women have not. This is true in part because women have often been excluded from the formal litanies of many churches and peoples. Such is not God's intent, nor the intent of God's church on earth. He intends that women claim, use, and rejoice in these gifts. This is affirmed in a revelation given to the Prophet Joseph Smith: "For what doth it profit a man [or woman] if a gift is bestowed upon him, and he receive not the gift? Behold, he rejoices not in that which is given unto him, neither rejoices in him who is the giver of the gift" (D&C 88:33).

Throughout the ages, prophets have testified of the

importance and availability of these gifts of the Spirit and of the benefits in their use. In his farewell testimony in the Book of Mormon, Moroni cautions us to "deny not the [spiritual] gifts of God, for they are many; and they come from the same God who worketh all in all; and they are given by the manifestations of the Spirit of God unto men, to profit them" (Moroni 10:8). Faith, wisdom, knowledge, personal revelation, a testimony of Jesus Christ, scriptural understanding, intuitive knowledge of your family's needs, healing; these are all gifts that are ours to claim. These are by no means all of the gifts, for the Lord has advised us that their number is infinite and their manifestation endless. Key to their possession, as mentioned, is that they are sincerely and righteously sought after, claimed, and used. Their acquisition and use adds important new dimension to our earthly spiritual growth, but for the Lord to thrust them upon you would be to deny you your agency.

The history of the Church is replete with examples of those who have been helped, protected, or have had lives spared as they have acted upon the promptings that come with such gifts. I'm sure each of you could relate such events that have taken place in your own or in your family's lives. Yet too often these stories go untold. These faith-promoting experiences need to be part of every family's dialogue.

THOUGHTS OF A LIVING PROPHET ON THIS SUBJECT.

Relating to the gifts of prayer and healing, President Gordon B. Hinckley, then first counselor in the First

Presidency, spoke of that dark chapter in our history known as the Haun's Mill Massacre:

"In that tragic happening Amanda Smith lost her husband and her son Sardius. Her younger boy Alma was savagely wounded. In the darkness she carried him from the mill to a shelter in the brush. His hip joint had been shot away. Through the night she cried out in prayer, 'Oh my Heavenly Father . . . what shall I do? Thou seest my poor wounded boy and knowest my inexperience. Oh Heavenly Father direct me what to do!' She later recorded in her journal concerning what happened: 'I was directed as by a voice speaking to me.

'The ashes of our fire [were] still smouldering. We had been burning the bark of the shag-bark hickory. I was directed to take those ashes and make a lye and put a cloth saturated with it right into the wound. It hurt, but little Alma was too near dead to heed it much. Again and again I saturated the cloth and put it into the hole from which the hip-joint had been ploughed. . . .

'Having done as directed I again prayed to the Lord and was again instructed as distinctly as though a physician had been standing by speaking to me. Near by was a slippery-elm tree. From this I was told to make a slippery-elm poultice and fill the wound with it.'

"She was able to get the injured boy to a house. With a mother's love and a mother's faith, she said to him, 'The Lord can make something there in the place of your hip.' She had him lie on his face, and there he remained while a

164

miracle occurred. Of that miracle she wrote, 'So Alma laid on his face for five weeks, until he was entirely recovered—a flexible gristle having grown in place of the missing joint and socket, which remains to this day a marvel to physicians.'"[2]

Alma's mother reported that Alma fully recovered, never limped, fulfilled a mission, and went on to live a rich, full life. All because a mother had the faith to take God at His word and to claim and act on gifts that He had told her were hers by right.

In another wonderful talk to women entitled "Ten Gifts from the Lord," President Gordon B. Hinckley, then second counselor in the First Presidency, enumerated some of the gifts of the Spirit that women particularly enjoy. Among those he listed were gifts of faith, prayer, discernment, and the power to heal. He recounted the story of Miriam in the Old Testament who was spoken of as a prophetess, reminding his listeners of the prophecy of Joel, as quoted by Peter in the New Testament: "And it shall come to pass in the last days, saith God, I will pour out of my Spirit upon all flesh: and your sons and your daughters shall prophesy, and your young men shall see visions, and your old men shall dream dreams: And on my servants and on my handmaidens I will pour out in those days of my Spirit; and they shall prophesy" (Acts 2:17–18). President Hinckley concluded his address by saying, "God bless you, my beloved sisters. . . . Please know that your place in the divine plan is no less important, no less great, and no less necessary than that of men. . . . Your potential is limitless. You are daughters of

God, endowed by inheritance with marvelous gifts and immeasurable potential."[3]

THE GIFT OF DISCERNMENT IS YOURS TO CLAIM

I grew up knowing that the gift of discernment and promptings by the Spirit could be mine and that the Lord did indeed convey to us those messages important to us, our families, and our welfare. My father spoke openly and naturally of the times that he was impressed to take a child to a hospital or to change a course of action to avoid danger or to rush out to help someone who was imperiled. He also spoke with example and faith of the reality of forces of evil and our right and privilege to discern their presence and of how to dispel them. Our home was filled with not just those of our faith but those of other faiths, who in times of trial or tragedy would come to him because they understood that he could offer them something of the Spirit, a complete understanding of which was unavailable in their own circle of experience.

My first recollection of the Spirit issuing a warning was during World War II. My sisters, who were en route to join their husbands who were stationed in the eastern United States, had been gone from our home for only a few hours when my mother said to me: "Your sisters are in danger and they need help." I didn't need to ask her how she knew. She called the Wyoming Highway Patrol and asked them to look for their car on the desolate stretch of road they would be crossing through on that blustery winter day. Just an hour later, they were found. Their car had slid on an icy spot and skidded down the roadside embankment. Had it not been for that prompting and Mother's willingness to act on it, they easily could have lost their lives to Wyoming's deadly winter.

Having witnessed in my early years several similar manifestations of the Spirit, I came to expect them to be a part of my life and found it natural to claim them and to act on them. During the years when our children were growing up, if the phone rang late at night, my husband's first response was, "Do we worry or don't we?" If the call told of someone being hurt or in an accident, he would say, "Do I run out in my robe, or do I have time to get dressed?" It became for us a way of lightly relieving tension in tight situations, but represented a deeper underlying trust. The Lord has been very generous with us and this gift, and we have had the confidence to rely on these promptings. In my international work with the diplomatic community for the Church, I have been led to key people, been removed from situations, have understood without knowing what was needed, and how to articulate those needs so as to have them properly understood, all because of this gift.

Spiritual promptings were openly acknowledged in our home in order that our children might also lay claim to them. Our son Tom returned from his mission to the Philippines with unusual stories of how heeding the promptings of the Spirit had saved his life. He told of being in the middle of a lesson with investigators in a particularly threatening part of a city when a voice clearly spoke to him and said, "You are to get up and leave, now." Without hesitation he did so. After leaving the house, he discovered that his companion had received the same prompting. They thought perhaps there was someone they should go find at that moment and diligently searched the surrounding streets. Finding no one, they returned to that humble home only to find no one was there. Neighbors told them that the police had arrived immediately after they left and had seized and removed the entire family. Tom and his companion would likely have been taken away as well, had they not heeded the warning so quickly. Though they tried, they were never able to find any trace of that family.

OUR RIGHT TO CLAIM THE GIFTS WAS ACQUIRED IN OUR PREMORTAL STATE

In an article entitled "The Origin of Man," published in 1909, the First Presidency of the Church declared that "man, as a spirit, was begotten and born of heavenly parents, and reared to maturity in the eternal mansions of the Father."[4] This statement supports what we earlier proposed—that Adam and Eve would have received in their premortal lives the training that qualified them to serve as the parents of the human race. It is reasonable to also assume that Adam and Eve and all their children (us) were sufficiently instructed and prepared to successfully wend our way through mortality and back to the presence of our heavenly parents. Given how quickly after birth children begin demonstrating individual personality traits, isn't it likely some of that development took place prior to our spirits taking up residence in our moral bodies? It is those unique abilities that will make it possible for us to fulfill our foreordained mortal missions.

We must claim those spiritual gifts to which we have a right and which are offered by a benevolent and loving God for our benefit, our edification, and our joy. We need to use them to the benefit of ourselves, our families, our church, and our communities. Lest those blessings be lost, we need to teach our children of their reality and of their right to also claim them.

Heed the words as recorded in Doctrine and Covenants concerning the use of these great gifts: "But a commandment I give unto them, that they shall not boast themselves of these things, neither speak them before the world; for these things are given unto you for your profit and for salvation" (D&C 84:73).

THE GREATEST SPIRITUAL GIFT— A SURE, STEADY FAITH

"Marvelous is the power of women of faith," President Hinckley testified. "It has been demonstrated again and again in the history of this church. It goes on among us today. I think it is part of the divinity within you."[5] However, we are reminded again and again that the greatest gift we can claim for ourselves and give to our families is a sure and steady faith, an unshakeable and absolute testimony of the divinity of the work, the divinity of the Savior and the divinity of each individual as a child of God. It is not in the spectacular moments of the Spirit that we define ourselves. It is by our staying power, our faith, and our generosity of self as we come face to face with the heady successes, heavy challenges, and quiet trials of our lives.

To claim and have a glorious spiritual gift does not mean that one will have courage for the long trek. Some of the most heartbreaking scriptural passages tell of those who received unusual gifts but could not bear the mundane, daily wrongs, hurts, and ambitions of self and others, and the temptations that bestrew their paths. The Lord has given us this latter-day warning: "For although a man may have many revelations, and have power to do many mighty works, yet if he boasts in his own strength, and sets at naught the counsels of God, and follows after the dictates of his own will and carnal desires, he must fall" (D&C 3:4).

> *IT IS NOT IN THE SPECTACULAR MOMENTS OF THE SPIRIT THAT WE DEFINE OURSELVES. IT IS BY OUR STAYING POWER, OUR FAITH, AND OUR GENEROSITY OF SELF.*

Not only must one be prudent in the use of one's gifts and boast of them not, It is also wise to be cautious as you claim those gifts. Elder Boyd K. Packer has advised us: "Be ever on guard lest you be deceived by inspiration from an unworthy source. You can be given false spiritual messages. There are counterfeit spirits just as there are counterfeit angels. (See Moro. 7:17.) Be careful lest you be deceived, for the devil may come disguised as an angel of light."[6]

Again we are reminded of the importance of holding to the iron rod, of staying the course, of remaining forever close and attuned to the Lord in all things. Salvation, redemption, and exaltation depend ultimately on our faith in the Savior Jesus Christ and His atonement

As you claim the gifts of the Spirit, let your testimony be strengthened by the testimonies of Joseph Smith and Sidney Rigdon:

> And now, after the many testimonies which have been given of him, this is the testimony, last of all, which we give of him: That he lives! For we saw him, even on the right hand of God; and we heard the voice bearing record that he is the Only Begotten of the Father—That by him, and through him, and of him, the worlds are and were created, and the inhabitants thereof are begotten sons and daughters unto God. (D&C 76:22–24)

THE PLAN IS PERFECT

And so we arrive at the point of beginning. With a clearer understanding of time, place, and space, the perfection of the plan emerges into clearer view. How enlightening it is to know with certainty that we are here on earth at exactly the right time. How empowering it is to come to understand that we have divine contracts to fulfill based on promises made in the eternities before. How ennobling to see that the great plan of happiness embraces all knowledge, sacraments, and ordinances that we will need to return safely home.

In the end, then, it all comes down to choices—our choices, our choice to honor our divine contracts, our choice to elect and select happiness, our choice of that which is vital over that which is merely important, our choice to embrace the Light of Christ, to invite the Holy Comforter into our lives, and to understand the true and very personal love of God for us.

In the end, it comes down to our choice to love and to sustain all those in our caring network and to fully honor the covenants and promises we have made to them, our choice to accept and to embrace the ordinances of the gospel and to be active participants the life of God's church on this earth, our choice to accept the loving support and enlightened guidance of the leaders of the Church, our choice to testify of Christ and embrace God's words, His works, and His plan.

We began these chapters with a triplet that was unfinished. Perhaps now is the time to finish it with an affirmation of our choices.

> I choose to think as God thinks—for there is light.
> I choose to love as God loves—for there is strength.
> I choose to live as God counsels me to live—for there is wholeness.
> I choose this day to move ever Eastward.

May you find unparalleled growth and unimagined joy in this, your mortal journey.

NOTES

NOTES TO PREFACE

1. Gaskill, *Lost Language of Symbolism*, 152.
2. Gaskill, *Lost Language of Symbolism*, 152.
3. See Gaskill, *Lost Language of Symbolism*, 149–51.
4. "East is the direction most often employed in the standard works of the Church. . . . In biblical Hebrew, the root *qdm* is the most common word-group meaning 'east.'" Gaskill, *Lost Language of Symbolism*, 150–51.
5. See Gaskill, *Lost Language of Symbolism*, 153.
6. See Campbell, *Eve and the Choice Made in Eden*, 70–72.

NOTES TO CHAPTER 1

1. "O My Father," *Hymns*, no. 292.
2. Nelson, *Power within Us*, 6.
3. Young, *Discourses of Brigham Young*, 392.
4. Maxwell, *Whom the Lord Loveth*, 123.

NOTES TO CHAPTER 2

1. See Smith, *Teachings of the Prophet Joseph Smith*, 365.
2. McConkie, *Mortal Messiah*, 1:23.
3. Snow, in *Journal of Discourses*, 14:302.
4. McConkie, *Mormon Doctrine*, 590.
5. McConkie, *Mormon Doctrine*, 290.
6. McConkie, *Mormon Doctrine*, 290.

7. Kimball, "The Role of Righteous Women," 102.
8. See Smith, *Teachings of the Prophet Joseph Smith,* 365.
9. Faust, "Heirs to the Kingdom of God," 63.
10. Top, "Foreordination," 523.
11. Holy Bible, New International Version, North American edition, International Bible Society.
12. Packer, "The Light of Christ."
13. *Messages of the First Presidency,* 5:3.
14. Peck, *Road Less Traveled,* 252.
15. Cannon, "Study and the Prayer of Faith," 87.
16. Young, *Manuscript History of Brigham Young,* 529.
17. Young, *Manuscript History of Brigham Young,* 529.
18. Wirthlin, "Unspeakable Gift," 27.
19. Tate, *Boyd K. Packer,* 64; emphasis added.
20. *Church News,* week ending December 4, 2004, 3.

NOTES TO CHAPTER 3

1. Maxwell, *That My Family Should Partake,* 86.
2. Smith, in *Journal of Discourses,* 25:57.
3. Maxwell, *One More Strain of Praise,* 107–8.
4. Maxwell, *One More Strain of Praise,* 104
5. Whitney, in Conference Report, April 1921, 32.
6. Top, *Life Before,* 152.
7. Top, *Life Before,* 152.

NOTES TO CHAPTER 4

1. Maxwell, *Lord, Increase Our Faith,* 49.
2. Maxwell, *Lord, Increase Our Faith,* 49.
3. Scott, "To Be Healed," 8.
4. Maxwell, *"Not My Will, But Thine,"* 119.
5. Maxwell, *Lord, Increase Our Faith,* 49.

NOTES TO CHAPTER 5

1. Widtsoe, *Evidences and Reconciliations,* 194.
2. Hinckley, "Rise to the Stature of the Divine within You," 96.
3. Kimball, *Writings of Camilla Eyring Kimball,* 60.
4. Hinckley, "Rise to the Stature of the Divine within You," 96.
5. Hinckley, "Women of the Church," 69.
6. Faust, "A Message to Our Granddaughters," 79.

7. Hinckley, "Building the Kingdom from a Firm Foundation," 10.
8. Quoted in *Great Quotes from Great Women*, 9.

NOTES TO CHAPTER 6

1. Madsen, "Emmeline B. Wells," 18–19.
2. Madsen, "Emmeline B. Wells," 18.
3. Maxwell, "Enduring Well," 8.
4. Keller, *Light in My Darkness.*
5. Young, in *Journal of Discourses*, 3:205–6.
6. Lincoln, *Writings of Abraham Lincoln*, 6:36.
7. Simmons, "But If Not . . . ," 75.
8. Author unknown, quoted in Kimball, *Faith Precedes the Miracle*, 99.
9. Faust, "A Time of Refining, Testing in Mortal Life," 4.
10. Maxwell, "'Swallowed Up in the Will of the Father,'" 23.
11. See Miller, "How Genes Affect Moods," 70.
12. Heaps, "Surviving the loss of a loved one to suicide," 11.

NOTES TO CHAPTER 7

1. Smith, *History of the Church*, 4:227.
2. Hinckley, *Standing for Something*, 3.
3. See Nelson, "Divine Love," 20.
4. Young, in *Journal of Discourses*, 4:216.
5. William Wordsworth, "Ode on the Intimations of Immortality," V, line 64.
6. Widtsoe, "Worth of Souls," 189.
7. Packer, "The Light of Christ."
8. *Hymns,* no. 308.

NOTES TO CHAPTER 8

1. Porter, "Cracked Looking-Glass."
2. Quoted in *Great Quotes from Great Women*, 12.
3. Bombeck, "If I Had My Life to Live Over."

NOTES TO CHAPTER 9

1. "The Family: A Proclamation to the World," 102.
2. *Teachings of Presidents of the Church: Harold B. Lee*, 148.
3. Hinckley, *Small and Simple Things*, 12.
4. Thanks to Dr. Phil McGraw for discussing a list on the *Oprah*

Show which contained some of these ideas and which served as a thought starter.

5. See Young, *Discourses of Brigham Young,* 416.
6. Ballard, *When Thou Art Converted,* 182.
7. Muir, *My First Summer in the Sierra,* 110.
8. Goodrich, "I Heard Him Come," 101.
9. Ballard, *When Thou Art Converted,* 58.
10. *Hymns,* no. 86.

NOTES TO CHAPTER 10

1. See *Ensign,* May 1995.
2. Hinckley, "Rise to the Stature of the Divine within You," 97.
3. Hinckley, "Ten Gifts from the Lord," 89.
4. "The Origin of Man," 80.
5. Hinckley, "Rise to the Stature of the Divine within You," 97.
6. Packer, "Candle of the Lord," 55–56.

SOURCES

—————

Ballard, M. Russell. *When Thou Art Converted: Continuing Our Search for Happiness.* Salt Lake City: Deseret Book, 2001.

Bombeck, Erma. "If I Had My Life to Live Over." In *Eat Less Cottage Cheese and More Ice Cream.* Kansas City, Mo.: Andrews McMeel Pub., 1979, 2003.

Campbell, Beverly. *Eve and the Choice Made in Eden.* Salt Lake City: Deseret Book, 2003.

Cannon, James W. "Study and the Prayer of Faith." In *Expressions of Faith: Testimonies of Latter-day Saint Scholars.* Edited by Susan Easton Black. Salt Lake City, Utah: Deseret Book and Provo, Utah: FARMS, 1996.

Church News, week ending December 4, 2004.

Ensign, May 1995.

"The Family: A Proclamation to the World." *Ensign,* November 1995, 102.

Faust, James E. "Heirs to the Kingdom of God." *Ensign,* May 1995.

———. "A Message to Our Granddaughters." In *Brigham Young University 1984–85 Devotional and Fireside Speeches.* Provo, Utah: Brigham Young University, 1985.

———. "A Time of Refining, Testing in Mortal Life." *Church News,* October 9, 2004.

Gaskill, Alonzo L. *The Lost Language of Symbolism: An Essential Guide for Recognizing and Interpreting Symbols of the Gospel.* Salt Lake City: Deseret Book, 2003.

Goodrich, Jeff. "I Heard Him Come." In *Top Fifty Songs from Your Favorite LDS Artists.* Salt Lake City: Deseret Book, 1997.

Great Quotes from Great Women. Compiled by Peggy Anderson. Franklin Lakes, N.J.: Career Press, 1997.

Heaps, Julie Dockstader. "Surviving the Loss of a Loved One to Suicide." *Church News,* March 13, 2004.

Hinckley, Gordon B. "Rise to the Stature of the Divine within You." *Ensign,* November 1989.

———. *Standing for Something: 10 Neglected Virtues That Will Heal Our Hearts and Homes.* New York: Random House, 2000.

———. "Ten Gifts from the Lord." *Ensign,* November 1985.

———. "Women of the Church." *Ensign,* November 1996.

Hinckley, Marjorie Pay. "Building the Kingdom from a Firm Foundation." In *As Women of Faith: Talks Selected from the BYU Women's Conferences.* Edited by Mary E. Stovall and Carol Cornwall Madsen. Salt Lake City: Deseret Book, 1989.

———. *Small and Simple Things.* Salt Lake City: Deseret Book, 2003.

Hymns of The Church of Jesus Christ of Latter-day Saints. Salt Lake City: The Church of Jesus Christ of Latter-day Saints, 1985.

Journal of Discourses, 26 vols. London: Latter-day Saints' Book Depot, 1854–86.

Keller, Helen. *Light in My Darkness.* 2d ed. West Chester, Pa.: Chrysalis Books, 2000.

Kimball, Camilla Eyring. *The Writings of Camilla Eyring Kimball.* Edited by Edward L. Kimball. Salt Lake City: Deseret Book, 1988.

Kimball, Spencer W. *Faith Precedes the Miracle.* Salt Lake City: Deseret Book, 1979.

———. "The Role of Righteous Women." *Ensign,* November 1979.

Lee, Harold B. *Teachings of Presidents of the Church: Harold B. Lee.* Salt Lake City: The Church of Jesus Christ of Latter-day Saints, 2000.

Lincoln, Abraham. *The Writings of Abraham Lincoln,* 8 vols. New York and London: G. P. Putnam's Sons, 1905–6.

Madsen, Carol Cornwall. "Emmeline B. Wells: A Fine Soul Who Served." *Ensign,* July 2003.

Maxwell, Neal A. "Enduring Well." *Ensign,* April 1997.

————. *Lord, Increase Our Faith*. Salt Lake City: Bookcraft, 1994.

————. *"Not My Will, But Thine."* Salt Lake City: Deseret Book, 1989.

————. *One More Strain of Praise*. Salt Lake City: Bookcraft, 1999.

————. "'Swallowed Up in the Will of the Father.'" *Ensign*, November 1995.

————. *That My Family Should Partake*. Salt Lake City: Deseret Book, 1974.

————. *Whom the Lord Loveth: The Journey of Discipleship*. Salt Lake City: Deseret Book, 2003.

McConkie, Bruce. R. *Mormon Doctrine*. 2d ed. Salt Lake City: Bookcraft, 1966.

————. *The Mortal Messiah: From Bethlehem to Calvary*. 4 vols. Salt Lake City: Deseret Book, 1979–81.

Messages of the First Presidency of The Church of Jesus Christ of Latter-day Saints. 6 vols. Compiled by James R. Clark. Salt Lake City: Bookcraft, 1965–75.

Miller, Michael C. "How Genes Affect Moods." *Newsweek*, December 8, 2003.

Muir, John. *My First Summer in the Sierra*. San Francisco, Calif.:" Sierra Club Books, 1998.

Nelson, Russell M. "Divine Love." *Ensign*, February 2003.

————. *The Power within Us*. Salt Lake City: Deseret Book, 1988.

————. "The Origin of Man," *Improvement Era*, November 1909.

Packer, Boyd K. "The Candle of the Lord," *Ensign*, January 1983.

————. "The Light of Christ." Address to mission presidents. Missionary Training Center, Provo, Utah, June 22, 2004, unpublished.

Peck, M. Scott. *The Road Less Traveled: A New Psychology of Love, Traditional Values, and Spiritual Growth*. New York: Simon and Schuster, 1978.

Porter, Katherine Anne. "The Cracked Looking-Glass." In *Collected Stories of Katherine Anne Porter*. Birmingham, Ala.: Southern Living Gallery, 1984.

Scott, Richard G. "To Be Healed." *Ensign*, May 1994.

Simmons, Dennis E. "But If Not . . ." *Ensign*, May 2004.

Smith, Joseph. *History of The Church of Jesus Christ of Latter-day*

Saints. Edited by B. H. Roberts. 2d ed. rev. 7 vols. Salt Lake City: The Church of Jesus Christ of Latter-day Saints, 1932–51.

————. *Teachings of the Prophet Joseph Smith.* Selected by Joseph Fielding Smith. Salt Lake City: Deseret Book, 1976.

Tate, Lucile C. *Boyd K. Packer: A Watchman on the Tower.* Salt Lake City: Bookcraft, 1995.

Top, Brent L. "Foreordination." In *Encyclopedia of Mormonism.* 4 vols. Edited by Daniel H. Ludlow. New York: McMillan, 1992.

————. *The Life Before: How Our Premortal Existence Affects Our Mortal Life.* Salt Lake City: Deseret Book, 1988.

Whitney, Orson F. In Conference Report, April 1921.

Widtsoe, John A. *Evidences and Reconciliations.* Arranged by G. Homer Durham. Salt Lake City: Bookcraft, 1960.

————. "The Worth of Souls," *Utah Genealogical and Historical Magazine,* October 1934.

Wirthlin, Joseph B. "The Unspeakable Gift." *Ensign,* May 2003.

Wordsworth, William. "Ode on the Intimations of Immortality." In *Seven Centuries of Verse.* Selected and edited by A. J. M. Smith. New York: Charles Scribner's Sons. 1957.

Young, Brigham. *Discourses of Brigham Young.* Selected and arranged by John A. Widtsoe. Salt Lake City: Deseret Book, 1954.

————. *Manuscript History of Brigham Young.* LDS Church Archives. Salt Lake City, Utah.

INDEX